CONTENT

Foreword   9

Introduction   11

0. First encounter with a child's suffering   15
Case study   15
The adult: a resonator   18
Children have strategies for healing themselves   19
First strategy: distancing oneself   19
Second strategy: enjoying the agreeable things that life continues to offer   20
Third strategy: looking suffering in the face   22
Have adults no part to play, then?   23
"You are bigger than your problems"   24
"But your problems are real problems!"   24
"I cannot share in your problems!"   25
THE GAMES MOTHERS PLAY   26
Things to talk about with your child   30

Part One

BEREAVEMENT

1. An unexpected death in the family   33
Case study   33
The difficulties experienced by adults   39
The adults were caring for a child in the abstract   39
Maybe the adults were still in their own "black hole"   41
Maybe they themselves were not prepared for death   41
Maybe they were too caught up in their own strategies   42
Children are aware of the solidarity network around them   43
A child is inclined to live fully in the present   44
Active and passive tasks   45
Environmental pollution   45
THE TOWN OF HEREAFTER   47
Things to talk about with your child   54

2. The danger of imprisoning a suffering child   55
Case study   55
Suffering out of loyalty …   61
… to a family system organised around grief   62
… to a family system where "everyone knows everything"   64
Choosing to have faith in life   65
WHAT DOES GRANDFATHER DO
    WITH GOD ALL DAY LONG?   67
Things to talk about with your child   72

WHEN CHILDREN SUFFER
Through Conflicts, Suffering & Loss

Mariateresa Zattoni & Gilberto Gillini

With a Foreword by
Eugenio Borgna and Franca Do

a Many Rooms publication

Published by **Many Rooms Publishing**

Copyright © 2002 Many Rooms Publishing

First published in 2000 in Italian under the title
PROTEGGERE IL BAMBINO

English translation by Simon Knight in association with
First Edition Translations Limited Cambridge UK

Cover: Orchid Design
Design: Rosemarie Pink

This edition printed July 2002

ISBN 0 85231 251 2

All rights reserved. No part of this publication may be reproduced, stored in a retrieval system, or transmitted in any form or by any means, electronic, mechanical, photocopying, recording or otherwise, without prior permission in writing from Many Rooms Publishing.

Printed by Polar Group Ltd Leicester LE4 9TZ

ManyRooms
PUBLISHING
Chawton   Hampshire   GU34 3HQ
Telephone 01420 88222   Fax 01420 88805
rp@ShineOnline.net   www.ShineOnline.net

3. Having to reconcile two mothers	73
Case study	73
How do I relate to my father's wife?	81
Acquiring new relatives without confusing existing ties	82
A conflict of loyalties	84
Unclear boundaries	85
Boundaries that cannot be crossed	86
Could there not be an alliance of mothers?	87
Confirmation from the Word of God	87
SEEING WITH YOUR EYES CLOSED	90
Things to talk about with your child	96

Part Two

GROWING PAINS

4. When suffering becomes a tyrant	99
Case study	99
Even the poisonous plant of guilt is a sign of love	
… which needs to be brought to the light	106
When religion adds to the sense of guilt	108
Defending oneself against the temptation to feel guilty	109
How to protect the child …	111
… and not rope others in	111
Who was there to help this family?	112
A CLEVER TRICK	113
Things to talk about with your child	118

5. When children have to "nurse" their parents 119
Case study 119
A vicious circle 123
When children are obliged to console their parents 124
Suffering is a precondition of maturity 127
The importance of establishing a proper distance 129
FIRST NIGHT AWAY FROM HOME 130
Things to talk about with your child 133

6. The sufferings of the adoptive child 135
Case study 135
The wound that cannot be denied 140
The trap of omnipotence 141
The trap of oversimplification 142
The trap of words 144
Who is the saviour? 146
SHARING A MOTHER HALF AND HALF? 147
Things to talk about with your child 151

Part Three

SUFFERING THAT CAN BE AVOIDED

7. When a child feels unwanted	155
Case study	155
Stop!	159
Let us try to understand the mother's loneliness and pain …	160
… as the soil in which her negative prophecy matures	161
Negative reactions	162
The absence of positive bonding with siblings	163
GRANDPARENTS ARE ALWAYS A GREAT ASSET	164
Things to talk about with your child	169

8. When one parent "steals" the other	171
Case study	171
How the father would defend his conduct	177
How the mother would defend her position	178
An egocentric, distorting filter	179
Taking sides for eternity	181
Ensuring real protection for the child	182
THE KEYBOARD	183
Things to talk about with your child	187

9. When a parent is impossible to please   189
Case study   189
When the family becomes a gas chamber ...   195
... without doors or windows giving access to other families   195
Three ways in which the care of a child becomes distorted   196
The child's real needs   197
Blaming oneself as a way of resolving the difficulty   198
A FULL AND COMPLETE LOVE   199
Things to talk about with your child   204

Afterword   205

Foreword

While leafing through Mariateresa Zattoni and Gilberto Gillini's book, I was reminded of the words of Charles Péguy: "There are tears which will last longer than the stars in the sky" – and this is true of the tears of children. But their tears can be wiped away by tender looks ... looks which, in them, "will shine eternally, night after night".

The sufferings of a child – the child we all bear within ourselves – will not be devastating if they are given a meaning (which need not be entirely clear), and if we do not fall into the pointless and arid trap of trying to explain everything.

We renew our encounter with ourselves day by day in the child we have been and are sensitive to the all-too-often mysterious suffering of our patients – patients who continue to suffer as a result of the things which, yesterday, made them vulnerable, distressed and/or sick.

A child never enters into suffering alone, not because this is a systematic viewpoint but because his or her individuality and ability to relate are defined in the encounter with the other. Psychological self-healing comes from the other; at the very dawn of life we encounter ourselves and bear with us the memory of that encounter.

It is nevertheless true that, though the encounter with the other is fundamental, we are not determined by it. There remains in us – vulnerable and susceptible to suffering though we may be – the possibility of redemption ("the most beautiful of all children is not yet born", according to the poet Hikmet) – the redemption of those freedoms that no suffering and/or therapeutic interpretation can take away.

This is the mystery of every human being – unique, unrepeatable, capable of the great step of reflection and awareness of his or her own existence.

Avoidable suffering assails us and continues to do so in the signs of psychic suffering, which often holds us back in a vice-like grip.

Our patients, their pain, our pain; with them we are on a pilgrimage. Suffering children all of us, we are learning how to work through suffering and, above all, how to try and understand.

This essay on the suffering of the child is also an invitation to have compassion on those who, inevitably, make and have made us suffer. Life repeats itself, once it becomes present and finds in the past and future of each person a root of hope and renewal. Let us be guided by the authors as they describe some fascinating case studies.

Prof. Eugenio Borgna*
Dr Franca Do**

---

*   Head of the Psychiatry Department at the Ospedale Maggiore, Novara, and lecturer at Milan University in the treatment of nervous and mental illnesses.
** Psychiatrist and psychotherapist.

Introduction

From the teacher's point of view, it is no easy matter to cover the very wide range of sufferings a child may have to undergo – sufferings which may relate to normal stages in his or her development, personal and social crises or, at worst, the experience of bereavement. We have tried to negotiate this "dark wood" with the light of hope, in the unshakeable belief that no one (least of all a child) should be asked to cope alone with totally devastating sufferings, and that in such sufferings there are always deeper meanings, though they may not be obvious and will need exploring.

This is not a treatise on child neuro-psychiatry, nor an essay on the pathologies of childhood, nor a text on the abuse and violence suffered by children. We have limited our investigation to the *normal sufferings* of a normal child in a normal family. Very little research has been done in this area, but we thought it needed exploring as a matter of urgency, because all too often parents are left to cope with their children's sufferings alone. We have limited our investigation to early and later childhood, up to the threshold of adolescence, and our emphasis throughout is that children never *enter* into suffering alone. There is a relationship – or several levels of relationship – in which they are engaged which offers them ways of responding to suffering, even though the people who are in relationship with them may not be aware of it. For this reason, we wanted to base our thinking not so much on a generalised child as on a particular child living in a particular family. This is not – and cannot be – a compendium of emergency solutions which tell you what to do in every single case.

Real-life events are instructive. By recounting them, we can enter into a situation and learn to respond to pain or, even better, activate the resources that a child has already internalised in order to cope with the pain of suffering. We in fact work from two basic premises, which inform the whole of our thesis. The first is based on the realisation that children learn from their environment and from their own inner resources to heal themselves. Accessing this means of psychological *self-healing* is a great step on the way to supporting them. It is also something that comes to us as a surprise. This is the purpose of the case studies of the section we have entitled Chapter Zero, where we set out the principle which will guide us throughout the book.

The second premise is that, even in the most terrible and unexpected situations, when suffering is absolutely inevitable, there is always a measure of suffering that is avoidable.

With this in mind, the text is divided into three parts.

In the first, we tackle sufferings (bereavements) in which the scope for avoiding suffering is minimal. But even learning to avoid this minimum of pain means equipping children so that they need not go defenceless into a situation that threatens to overwhelm them.

In the second section, the margin of avoidability is that much greater. In particular, the sufferings associated with growing up and the accidents which occur along the way can be alleviated by sensitive behaviour on the part of the adults concerned.

The sufferings dealt with in the third section would seem to be completely or very largely avoidable. We are concerned here with sufferings inflicted (for the most part unwittingly) on the child. By becoming at least partially aware of them we should be able to take preventive measures. This is possibly the most "painful" part of the book, because it asks us adults to face up to our mistakes, but it also urges us to hope for better things.

The central part of each chapter is a *reflection/essay* on how to support the child in his or her suffering. This is introduced by a *case study* and followed by a section entitled *Let me tell you a story* …

The introductory section is not just an anecdotal introduction (which could be skipped by the hurried reader wanting to get straight to the heart of the problem), but the solid foundation on which the subsequent thinking is based, anticipating the various strands of the argument. Our experience is that reflection and technical analysis, inevitably consisting of abstractions, can easily be ambiguous or melt away without trace. This is far less likely to happen if we have the courage to get to grips with a real, concrete situation.

The final section (*Let me tell you a story* ...) is addressed to the suffering child. The language and situations are geared to his or her level of understanding. This section is also a vital part of the process and should not be skipped, because it shows how good can come out of the most distressing situation. The adult reader, too, can be helped to understand how just a small step on his or her part can help put the child's suffering in perspective. Adults can use this child-centred story to help the child, and maybe follow the leads offered by the questions printed at the end (*Things to talk about with your child*). But first they should let themselves be energised by the sense of hope.

Who can read this book with profit? Parents, of course, but we hope it will also be useful to those with a professional concern. Teachers, educators, social workers, volunteers and catechists will be able to use the material provided in the story to get alongside children in difficult and painful situations.

Chapter Zero

First encounter with a child's suffering

Case study

In the great city of Milan, I had rented a bed-sitter, high up on the fourth floor, with no lift. I was a student at the time, and still quite unaware of the joys – and wisdom – a child can bring. One day, I was climbing the stairs, loaded with shopping, when I came face to face with the suffering of a child. On the top step leading to the second-floor door, a little stranger was sitting, as if a mountain had collapsed on top of him. He was wearing only socks on his four-year-old feet, clasping his arms round his knees and staring straight in front of him. His face was as immobile and pale as the surface of the moon. The door behind him was closed tight shut. It looked huge, faded and forbidding, quite unlike mine – so modest and welcoming – two floors higher up.

"Hello," I said.

He made no reply. As well as my bags, I carried a weighty question up to the fourth floor with me: why had that child been exiled? Half an hour later, the burdensome question brought me down again, because the unhappy expression of the child gave me no peace as I arranged my books on my table.

He was still there, not having moved at all. Of course, he did not know me, new tenant that I was; and I had no idea of the identity of this foundling-exiled-punished-expelled-forgotten-invisible child.

"Who are you waiting for?" I hazarded with forced cheerfulness.

"No one," he sighed.

"What's your name?"

Silence. You do not give your name away to strangers!

I sat down, adopting the same attitude as the child, but overcoming the temptation to take off my shoes. I was met with a surprised, sideways glance.

"Have you a family?" I asked again.

"No."

I seemed to have got it wrong, as if I were suspecting that he had no family! I needed to reformulate the question. "Where is your family?"

It worked. The child pointed to the big, faded, mean-looking door.

"Why don't you go in?"

After a pause, he said: "I've got a new little sister."

In a flash I understood it all. It was as if he had said: "It's the enemy, the usurper, a whole army of enemies, defeat, unconditional surrender, ultimate defeat."

Without the least regard for the fact that it was no concern of mine, and without asking his permission, I took him in my arms, while he – little man – dissolved into undignified tears. I rang the bell and knocked for good measure, in a state of agitation.

"Your child is out here crying!" I almost shouted at the person who came to open the door. And at the same time I was met with celebratory chatter, noise, music and exchanges of compliments.

I thought they must be monsters: how could they be celebrating while a little child was overwhelmed with suffering?

The boy who had opened the door laughed: "It wasn't us who told him to go out!"

Meanwhile, I could hear the words of a group of women, sharp as razor-blades. "What a little darling! At last, they've got the little girl they wanted!"

"Oh, what a perfect little nose! She's going to have lovely hair when she grows up. You can tell from the dark down on her head."

"Yes, she'll make the boys' heads turn. Good for her!" chimed in another, as a faint smile passed over the face of the new baby.

"Hey! There you are, Nico! Come and give your little sister a kiss!" Another woman had became aware of the presence of my "prey" and took him from my arms. Nico – now I knew his name – stiffened, clenched his teeth and pushed her away with his fists.

"Now you're no longer Mummy's darling!" she remarked, moved, it seemed to me, by some irrepressible sadistic impulse. And at the same time, heedless of the child's attempts to get away, she held him casually over the cradle so that his lips touched the cheek of the sleeping baby. Taken by surprise, Nico went through the motions of giving her a kiss, while maintaining his sulky, hurt look.

I felt as if I had stumbled into a den of insensitive, heartless cannibals.

How can one not be aware of the sufferings of a child? How is it possible to treat a child so badly? How is it possible to go into raptures over a new baby and completely forget another little human being weighing not a great deal more? I was so young, I could hardly face up to such a bunch of monsters. There was one thing I could do, though, almost as a challenge.

"Could Nico come up and play with me for a bit? I'm ..."

"... the young student lady!" laughed a woman in a pink dressing-gown, whom I at last identified as the mother. And so I realised that I had already been "sighted".

I took my new friend up to the fourth floor, where I told him stories and fed him chocolates. Then, just as I was thinking it would be a tough job to persuade him to go home, I realised that getting him to go back would be quite painless; he needed no prompting at all.

The adult: a resonator

I can now clearly identify – and smile at – the many mistakes I made in that far-distant encounter with a child's suffering.

It is easy to list the more superficial of them. I identified too closely with him, taking his side by gut reaction and effectively saying: "You are right to feel so hurt. You have experienced a great misfortune: the birth of a little sister! And you are even more unfortunate in having monsters for parents, insensitive brothers and relatives. Poor Nico!"

Of course, the Nico in question took full advantage of my partisan reaction: he let me spoil him, gained an enthusiastic narrator of fairy stories, and stuffed himself with chocolates. A good thing I was only "the young student lady", and so was not in a position to do him much harm (as we shall see, this often happens when an adult takes on board and amplifies a child's sufferings, acting rather like a resonator).

Then I had intruded on a party for a new-born baby. I was not ejected – thanks to the good manners of those good, kind people – but my attitude was undoubtedly judgemental. Was I really in a position to assess how those adults were behaving in fussing over the new baby and "ill-treating" poor little Nico – abandoning him to his suffering? The question of intrusion is another matter I shall have more to say about later on.

But the less obvious error I want to bring to light was my inability to understand how a child is able to heal himself.

Children have self-healing strategies which adults are in danger of upsetting and cancelling out, whether they are detached and brisk or overly sensitive and interventional (the two opposing poles tend to meet).

Learning to respect a child's "inner healer" is an important and difficult lesson.

But we can be quite sure that this inner healer exists, lulled to sleep or drugged though it may be as a result of adult intrusions. Only children who have been seriously abused from a very early age and totally under the thumb of sadistic adults are incapable of reawakening their inner healer; and in this case they will exhibit a completely crushed and lost attitude, so frightfully inert and passive as to be the greatest moral slap in the face to any adult: "Hit me, then; I know you're right."

But unless they have reached so dreadful a level of annihilation, children have the inner resources to heal themselves. It is the role of adults to recognise and respect them.

Children have strategies for healing themselves
First strategy: distancing oneself
Let us now take a slow-motion look at the self-healing procedures followed by little Nico. First, he slips away from the party – apparently unobserved – chooses exile and sits down alone on the stairs. He gives himself a moment's pause to experience his suffering more fully ("I'm not going back in," "My place has been usurped," "Daddy and Mummy don't love me any more; they love her") and, at the same time, to reassure himself that he can cope on his own

("OK, I'll manage without them," "I'm grown up"). He takes a break, tries to understand himself.

So, the first method for the inner healer is to distance oneself from the immediacy of suffering.

The party going on in there is something so crushing; not being the centre of attention is so disastrous for the little egocentric, that he prefers to spend time alone. The child who temporarily distances himself is a child intent on healing himself, looking for a way to avoid being crushed.

Second strategy: enjoying the agreeable things that life continues to offer

Naturally, little Nico has not foreseen the arrival of a "Good Samaritan" coming up the stairs. His first instinct is therefore to exclude her. His attitude is a way of saying: "It's nothing to do with you." But since she is in no doubt about his immediate need of help and offers him warmth, protection and partisan support, Nico takes healthy advantage of the fact. He allows her to take up his cause, tell him stories and stuff him with chocolates.

Let it be said immediately that when adults think they have uncovered the hidden meanings of a child's behaviour, they are probably projecting their own motives and manoeuvres – what they would do if they were in the child's shoes. If adults were to say: "That's why Nico has taken up exile on the stairs, because he is seeking attention!" (and, in this case, Nico's willingness to be petted by the Good Samaritan would be proof of his hidden intention!), they would probably be speaking about themselves, not about Nico. They would be revealing what they, adults – able to act on more than one level – would do. But children are always an undivided whole in the actions they perform; they are always whole-heartedly involved in what they do, without ulterior motives. In the first flowering of adolescence – which in some respects occurs very precociously in our culture – children become capable of such double dealing, of acting on two levels. They have learned from adults that factual reality (crying) and intentions (the advantage to me of crying) do not necessarily correspond. New horizons open up to them; they can see reality from various points of view. And this opens the way to new resources.

Returning to Nico, let us say that he eventually accepts the unexpected presence of the Good Samaritan and allows himself to be consoled.

This is a second self-healing strategy: suspending one's suffering, allowing oneself to be comforted, taking "what comes along" if it offers consolation.

Parents are often alarmed by this sort of attitude on the part of children: "What! A moment ago they seemed to be hurting badly and now they've forgotten all about it?" and – adopting the strange human strategy of wanting to bring everything down to their own level of understanding – instead of being pleased that the children are comforted, present them with the "bill" for their suffering. It is as if they were saying: "But if you were so unhappy, how can you be enjoying yourself so soon afterwards? How can you be taking an interest in fairy stories and chocolates if you are so hurt? Someone who is so quickly comforted is incapable of real suffering ..." We know of a father who took his daughter to the cemetery to visit her mother's grave because she had not mentioned her mother in the previous week! This ability to be easily comforted, this intermittent kind of suffering (while looking at my little sister, I am hurting; while eating chocolates, I am enjoying myself), seems inconsistent to adults, whose awareness of themselves is a seamless whole, sharp and linear, easily transformed into a prison. A nine-year-old girl "presumed" – the word used by her mother – to make her mother happy by giving her a red scarf, when she – recently widowed – was supposed to dress in black. This red scarf, given to her mother on the girl's return from a school trip, was proof that she was insensitive, "too" intent on her games and amusements. "You could hardly expect me to buy a black scarf!" protested the girl, but the mother took this as further proof that her daughter was incapable of understanding.

On the contrary, an easy transition from moments of pain to moments of joy is a precious sign: the child is not living in the land of suffering. The child does not feel at home there and – healthily – grasps at any handhold that will enable him or her to escape. Adults permitting.

Somehow another – ancient – wisdom is written on his or her heart: human beings are not made for suffering; suffering cannot be transformed into a grave that one digs with one's own hands.

Suffering is to be escaped from, with strategies not considered by adults, who – with the very best of intentions – cannot impose their methods of consolation. If our dear old friend Fido has died, and the child is inconsolable, it is pointless offering to go and buy a replacement, because the child knows perfectly well that Fido cannot be cloned. But if adults will just hold back from protecting the child from his or her hurt, they may be in for a surprise. The Good Samaritan was surprised that – in the end – she did not need to take Nico back home against his will; he was ready to go with no prompting.

Third strategy: looking suffering in the face

It is possible to imagine Nico returning home when the party was over and – unbeknown to anyone else – going to take a peek at his little sister, dismayed to find his rival with "no teeth, a big mouth and unable to talk" (the consoling portrait that the little boy might give his sister).

We can be certain that when a child looks suffering in the face, it is because he or she is in some way ready to cope with it, even when to a third party it seems an immense burden. "If you do not give me my first communion soon, it will be too late," said seven-year-old

Michael one day to his friend the priest: it was his way of looking straight at his imminent death from AIDS. He was ready to face up to death – far more ready than everyone else around him. We also need to have a sense of the right moment.

Have adults no part to play, then?

This is a vital question: if children are able to heal themselves, what is the role of parents and educators – in a word, the adults who are close to them? Should they perhaps leave them alone? Should they respect them to the point of taking no interest at all?

The question would be better put in another way: what adult–child relationship best promotes the process of self-healing?

Under the first formulation of the question lies the fear of not having any part to play, being superfluous to requirements, reduced to the role of spectator. But there is no such role. Instead, there are endless possible ways of relating which can help or hinder a process – in our case the stirring of the child's own self-healing ability or resources.

The second formulation of the question is therefore more relevant and "scientific".

The parent–educator is never on holiday, never a mere spectator.

I am not saying this to cultivate guilt complexes (if I get involved, something is bound to go wrong!) or perhaps drive people to take refuge in a depressive "I've done it all wrong", but to improve our chances. Some of our attitudes as parents are spontaneous and need to be reinforced, recognised as naturally good. It is far better to reinforce these attitudes than to "cry over spilt milk". It is far more useful to strengthen what we are already doing right than engage in breast-beating over our failures.

"You are bigger than your problems"

Let us try and learn another lesson from the story of Nico, immersed in his domestic drama. The woman (presumably his aunt) who held him over the cradle so that he could kiss his little sister – despite his sulky expression and rigid body language – seems to be saying: "This suffering is something you can cope with. A little sister is not the ultimate disaster, you know. I am sure that, really, you love your little sister." Since she is intimately convinced of this (though probably not in a very conscious way), she does not doubt that Nico will give his sister a kiss.

And she was right. To the great surprise of the Good Samaritan, Nico did proffer the expected kiss. It is true that the aunt's next remark "Now you are no longer Mummy's darling", seems gratuitous, slightly sadistic, something the aunt could have left unsaid. But what really mattered was the non-verbal aspect of it, the tone and the gestures with which the words were spoken. If the aunt's demeanour was warm and joyful, it could even be interpreted as: "Now you are a big boy."

Nico's relatives, then, establish a relationship with him which conveys the message: "You are bigger than your problems," "Your minor/major suffering is not the end of the world," "I know you'll get over it." Relational prophecies of this kind are very important in arousing his inner healer.

"But your problems are real problems!"

This has nothing to do with denying the child's suffering – or not allowing that what has happened is a genuine reason for suffering. If the adult's attitude is to be healthy, he or she needs to make contact with the inner world of the child and allow it to exist. This is the approach that will trigger the child's self-healing strategies.

But why would adults ever want to deny a child's sufferings? Why would they be so stupid as to say to the child: "You are being silly! This is no reason to suffer! If you are going to be so silly ..." How can adults fail completely to see a child's pain, be completely blind to his or her sufferings? How can they look at the child and in fact see someone else – see the image of the child they have in their mind – and not be aware of the signals coming from the real child?

There are many ways of answering this question. Suffice it to say that adults who are closed to a child's sufferings are adults who are defending themselves, self-centred, completely focused on their own affairs and duties. Acknowledging the sufferings of the child in their charge would tend to wipe out their reference points and sense of security, the formulae in which they believe.

The healthy, flexible adult, on the other hand, will allow the child to experience his or her suffering, knowing – as we said earlier – that it will not crush the child. By so doing, the adult provides the reassurance and support that will activate the child's own resources.

"I cannot share in your problems!"

The gut reaction that adopts an interactive approach – "My child, I experience your sufferings as if they were my own and I stand in your place to nullify them and drive them away" – conveys an opposite message to the child: "This suffering may crush you," "You can't cope." It is akin to my attitude as the Good Samaritan in the case of Nico. I had no doubt about what the child was feeling and was very aware of the insensitivity of those who "ought to" have been protecting him. Of course, "the young lady from upstairs" was of no real importance in the life of the child but, if she had been the mother, an aunt or a grandparent, an intrusion of this kind could have had enormous consequences. Sooner or later, the child would have become convinced of the opposite of the message being conveyed to console and protect him: that he could not cope. And his feelings, words and actions would have been conditioned by the experience of the adults he took his cue from. His inner healer would have remained inert, basically because there was no need of it.

We will examine these distancing or intrusive approaches in greater depth as we investigate the ways in which a child's suffering is expressed.

Let me tell you a story ...

The games mothers play

There was once a child who had no mother. It was not that his mother did not exist, but she had gone into hospital for two weeks, then she would be back. But Luke did not understand this. Everybody around him understood it and was in no doubt about it. But, for Luke, only one thing was clear: his mother had disappeared. Before, his mother had been there with him. She prepared his food, rejoiced at every new word he learned, and put his pyjamas on before he went to bed. Luke remembered these things very clearly.

But his mother had disappeared.

Luke toddled round the house, saying aloud the word "Fish", clearly enunciating the final "sh". Perhaps his mother would pop up and say: "Good boy!" His aunt, though, who was trying to find her way around the kitchen, appeared at the door and asked: "What's all this about fish? Where have you seen a fish?"

Luke, who was only just two, did not reply. The word had just popped out, carefully pronounced and shining bright; perhaps it would have the power to call up his mother. She would have stopped everything she was doing to come and give him a hug and say: "Good boy!" She would not have asked that sort of question.

But the word "fish" had not caused his mother to materialise.

Nor did the word "bababoo", which in any case had no meaning. His father even gave him a mild telling-off: "Whatever do you mean? That's baby talk."

At this point, Luke made a great effort and, with intense concentration and summoning up all his resources, made the longest speech of his life: "Where Mummy?"

His father understood immediately. His two-year-old son was missing his mother.

"She's in hospital, as you know," he replied affectionately, without giving the matter much thought. "She'll be home in a fortnight, three weeks at the most. I can't take you into her ward because children are not admitted, and she can't walk yet. Be patient, little man, she'll be back."

Luke understood not a word but, not wanting to annoy his father, replied with a serious: "Yes."

However, he could not suppress a sigh, which brought a smile to his father's lips.

"I'm missing Mummy, too," he added, as if he were speaking to an equal.

Luke went and stuck his head between his father's knees, gently rocking backwards and forwards, and his father was sure they had understood each other.

As the days went by – incredible though it may seem – the vivid memories of his mother gradually faded in little Luke's mind.

At first, he seemed to hear her voice, sometimes even feel her warmth when he hid in his bed in the hope that she would come and find him. But as the memories lost their colour, a hole began to open up in his heart. He did not know why, but gradually he lost his appetite. Before he had been a big eater; now he was fussy. He left food on his plate, even though his aunt made an effort to prepare the meals he liked.

And everyone was aware of the change in his appearance. He had become rather pale and very pensive. If you could ignore the softness of his skin and his natural chubbiness, you would have said he looked like an adult immersed in deep meditation.

"Are you all right?" his father would ask.

"Yes," answered Luke, or sometimes he made no reply at all.

Then one day he heard his mother's voice on the telephone. It was really her. It was really her voice. If he had been a puppy, he would have started wagging his tail with delight, as he held the receiver in his hand. He would have put his head back and barked with joy.

Instead, Luke just stood there with the handset in his hand, enchanted, his eyes open wide, absorbed in his happiness, but he said nothing: "Darling? Can you hear me? It's Mummy!" said the voice. Luke glued the handset to his ear, as if he wanted to hug it and never let it go.

"Luke, darling ..." said the voice.

"Say hello to Mummy!" urged his father, who was also bewildered by his son's bewilderment. "Say hello!"

Luke made the gesture of hello with his hand and continued to look with wonder at the telephone handset.

His father then took the handset back and continued his conversation with his wife, reassuring her that Luke had heard what she had said.

That day, Luke cleared his plate in a flash.

Next morning, just as Luke's father was leaving for the office, he observed something most unusual: Luke had climbed up on a chair, had lifted the telephone handset and was licking it.

"Whatever are you up to?" asked his father in amazement. "Why aren't you in bed with your aunt?"

Luke, still in his pyjamas, was off in a flash, back to his bed, where his aunt was still sleeping.

All day, his father remembered the bizarre occurrence and could not work it out in his mind.

Next day, he saw Luke lick the telephone handset again.

Meanwhile, Luke's complexion was returning to normal, and his absorbed expression had almost disappeared. If only his father had been able to get inside Luke's head for a moment, he would have learned that mothers can transform themselves into telephone handsets.

Better a telephone-mummy than no Mummy at all.

In fact, when his mother at last reappeared in flesh and blood, standing at the front door, face radiant and arms outstretched towards him, Luke first glanced at the telephone, as if to say: "But hadn't you turned into the handset?"

His doubts lasted only a moment, then Luke threw himself into her arms, mumbling the incomprehensible words that bubbled up from his happy little soul.

The games mothers play!

But when they come back, they are even more beautiful than before.

> ***Things to talk about with your child***
> – How did Luke "hold out" until his mother came back?
> – Why did he lick the telephone? Was it perhaps a way of "healing himself" of her absence?

PART ONE

BEREAVEMENT

In this section, we shall be examining a form of suffering that it is absolutely impossible to avoid: bereavement. Some events come upon us out of the blue and all we can do is come to terms with them. Children, too, may be affected by the death of a person dear to them, possibly the death of someone to whom they are very attached and who represents their security, their life-line. What is avoidable in such situations?

It would seem that the most the adults responsible for the child can do is to teach him or her resignation and, of course, do all they can to alleviate the pain of the child's loss.

However, in the stories of Albert, Martina and Luke, we shall see that part of their sufferings could have been avoided. We shall be examining not only strategies to ensure that the child's suffering is not completely overwhelming and – most important of all – to awaken his or her capacity for "self-healing", but also some of the wrong patterns of behaviour that adults may adopt when there is a bereavement. These include the tendency to project their own suffering onto the child, the rigid expectation of certain signs of pain which the child "ought to feel", the need (felt by adults) to "freeze" the onward flow of life, and an inability to recognise the child's independent strategies for coping with his or her suffering.

In particular, we shall be suggesting answers to the questions that inevitably arise. How can a child bear the sudden death of his or her father? What should one say to the child? Is it a good idea to let the child see the dead body? Can the child come to an adequate understanding of death?

What help should be given to a child who sees his or her mother fall ill and die? Who can take the place of the mother? And in what way? How can you tell if a child is unable to cope with his or her suffering? Is it right that the child should have another mother? On what conditions will the child be able to accept her?

Chapter One

An unexpected death in the family

Case study

Albert had recently started at primary school. It was all new to him, as he had not attended nursery school with any regularity. But in the evening, when his father came home, he took great pride in showing him his exercise-book, already "dog-eared" (as he put it), marked with the saliva where he had tried to cross out his crossings-out and splashed with bright colours which had a habit of trespassing beyond the squares intended to discipline his efforts. Underneath his drawings his first words were featured, written in big letters which also tended not to respect the squares on the page. His father would marvel at his work and say: "Magnificent!", as if it were the first time he had seen words illustrated in this way. And if Albert was able to make out what he had written, his father – with a strange catch in his voice – would look at his wife and say: "He's going to be a scholar!" – by which perhaps he meant someone who uses his brain, not someone who has to struggle with reinforced concrete for a living.

It was a Tuesday. When Albert rubbed the sleep from his eyes, on a cold, wintry morning, his father (Attilio) had already left for the building site. But when Albert came home at lunch-time, he found his grandmother there. Nothing unusual about that: three days a week his mother went to do housework for a lady and did not get back until three o'clock. On that Tuesday, though, his mother did not come home. His grandmother had an absent look, as if she were lost in thought. It did not escape Albert that she ran to the telephone the moment it rang. But she said nothing to him. The house was strangely silent. Albert did not even ask if he could go out and play with his friends.

Then an aunt arrived, his mother's sister: "What news, then?"

"Nothing," said his grandmother.

Some neighbours also arrived: "Any news?"

"Nothing definite yet," said his grandmother.

Albert became increasingly fearful and retreated into his exercise-book, chewing his pencil.

His grandmother prepared some soup, which they ate as the house gradually filled with people.

"Mummy will be back late, because your daddy is very ill."

"Where is Mummy?" asked Albert.

"She's at the hospital with your dad. Now it's time to say a prayer for your mother."

"And for Daddy," Albert added immediately.

"Quite right!" said his grandmother, almost with a smile.

When Albert woke up next morning, there were even more people in the house.

"In a minute your father will be arriving," said his maternal aunt, taking him in her arms.

"At last!" exclaimed the child.

"But he'll be in a big wooden box."

"Why?" asked Albert in amazement.

"Because he is dead," said his aunt, bursting into tears.

"Can we take him out of the box?" was Albert's immediate question.

But his aunt put him down and handed him on to his grandmother, who was crying even more than she was. There was also a nun there, whom he had never seen before, because "his" nun from nursery school had gone away. While shaking hands with his grandmother, the nun said to him: "Now your father is watching you from heaven."

Albert did not understand, he was so confused.

Finally, his mother arrived, worn out, dazed and upset. She picked him up, but in an almost mechanical way, while continuing to dab at her tears with a handkerchief. They were all talking about an accident, planks, scaffolding, death, fate. Everyone had an opinion about what should have been done, why there was no safety equipment, why they had operated on him, why they had sent him straight home.

Meanwhile, a big wooden box stood there, cold and silent.

"That's where your daddy is, in there," said one of his aunts, noticing that he had begun to circle round it.

Albert "saw" his father, two evenings before, sitting next to him on the settee and saying, in his usual enthusiastic way, "Magnificent!" as he looked at his exercise-book. He could not imagine that he was there in the box, dead. The priest arrived, accompanied by the smell of candles, rosaries, lowered voices and tears. The few people who took any notice of Albert said things like: "Eat", "Don't cry" (he was not crying anyway), "Your daddy is in heaven now and he will always protect you." His little mind tried to take it all in: an overwhelming wave of words and gestures. He distinctly heard his (maternal) aunt say to his grandmother: "I don't know how that woman there has the gall to turn up after the way she made her brother suffer." The woman in question was an aunt on his father's side, with whom – as Albert remembered very clearly – his father had often quarrelled on the telephone. And then his other grandmother was there (the one he hardly ever saw), weeping in a corner and reciting her rosary, saying nothing, even when someone offered their condolences. And again, he heard his aunt say: "Why is she crying now? She shouldn't have thrown him out!"

Two days after the funeral, his mother took him to school. The teacher who helped him learn to write kissed him, took him in her arms (to his great embarrassment), then set him down at his desk, gently, delicately, as if he were now made of glass. His companions formed a tight group around him. Fortunately they did not talk about wooden boxes, heaven or the cemetery. A little girl took from her pocket a chocolate egg wrapped in bright-yellow paper, half-squashed but none the less tempting. When, in later life, Albert thought of the word "consolation", he always had a mental image of that yellow-wrapped chocolate egg and the half-smile, half-grimace of his little friend as she offered it to him. Her gift was followed by others, all given in silence. The egg was joined on his desk by a pencil-sharpener (oh, how it appealed to him), a sheet of light-blue paper, a toy soldier, a model car (weren't they banned at school?), a doughnut and lots of other nice things, while the teacher – also silent – took out a Kleenex tissue, as if she had a bad cold.

During morning break, everyone said to him: "Do you want to play with me?"

Albert was extraordinarily calm. When it was time to draw, he drew with all the others. When it was time to copy words from the blackboard, he did the same as everyone else. At the same time, he could feel the teacher's gaze upon him.

One day, while he was looking at his exercise-book and everyone was busy drawing, Albert cried out: "Magnificent!"

And he smiled. The teacher looked at him in astonishment; she was not aware of anything particularly magnificent. This bizarre incident was repeated at intervals.

As a result, one day the teacher for reading, in consultation with her colleagues, sent for Albert's mother.

"We are very worried about Albert."

"Why, what has he been doing?" asked his mother in surprise.

"That's the point. He hasn't been doing anything, as if he were unconcerned by the bereavement. We just wanted to know how he is behaving at home. Is he ever dejected? Does he ask about his father?"

"I've never really seen him dejected," said his mother. "The first few days, he would ask where his father had gone and, when I said 'to heaven', he was just quiet. There's nothing unusual about his behaviour, as far as I can tell."

"There's one thing he does that's rather odd," said the teacher. "Sometimes – and my colleagues tell me this, too – he looks at his exercise-book and says 'Magnificent!', shouting the word in an enthusiastic way, just like that."

"Now you mention it, at home he sometimes calls out: 'Put that here' or 'Don't do that.' I've heard him say such things myself."

"Could he be thinking of his father?"

"Yes, I think so. Yesterday, an aunt phoned and asked if he wanted to go round to her house to play and he answered: 'Daddy doesn't want me to,' and was determined not to go. Then his other grandmother rang up and said, 'I'll make you some pancakes,' but he didn't want to go." His mother added: "In any case, he's right – they never took any interest before, so now we'll let things stay as they were," and an extraordinary hardness came over her face.

"My daddy has gone away like Liz's daddy," Albert told his mother one day.

"Who told you so?" asked his mother, who knew that Liz's parents had separated.

"He told me, in secret."

"And what else did Liz tell you."

"Nothing."

"What do you mean, nothing? Didn't he tell you that his daddy went away because he didn't love him any more?"

"No, that's not true. His daddy loves him very much. My daddy loves me, too."

"So why did Liz's daddy go away?"

"He just went away."

"But your daddy hasn't gone away. He was killed, poor man, in an accident."

"It doesn't make any difference," answered Albert with a frown.

The difficulties experienced by adults

In recounting this (true) story, we have taken the side of Albert, practically crying out on his behalf "against life", because it has robbed him of his father, and crying out against the adults for leaving him alone and proving incapable of helping him in his suffering.

But however strongly we feel, we have to admit that it is difficult for adults to play an adequate role in such circumstances. In this case, they have committed mistake after mistake. Unfortunately, there is no guidebook advising adults on how to cope with a funeral in the family; and even if there were a publication of this kind, it would be useless: it could only describe the suffering of one generalised child on the death of a parent, not the particular suffering of the particular child in question.

The adults were caring for a child in the abstract

Let us learn from Albert. To an outsider (but it is very difficult for close relatives to realise it), it is clear that Albert is not yet ready for a final separation from his father. And in any case, does life demand it of him? Where is it written that he must understand death straight away?

The adults around him expect him to feel a degree of pain: a child whose father has died ought to cry, be dejected, call out for him and rebel; he should miss his father and be unable to concentrate at school. We all have a mental picture of what suffering entails, a sequence of actions that "ought to" happen and that would to some extent reassure the adults concerned.

A child who, immediately after a bereavement, asks few questions and is able to pay attention at school and play is a perplexing phenomenon; and indeed, the teachers and his mother are disturbed by it. Why? Maybe because – without intending to – the child robs them of the task of "consoling" him. When a bereavement of such serious impact occurs, adults tend to dredge up a string of consoling ideas borrowed from popular psychology: your daddy has gone to heaven, he is always near you, he sees and protects you; now you must not cry, you must become a little man and so on. If children fail to exhibit the grief that adults expect of them, it is most likely they will have feelings of anxiety. And then there is the danger that they will put the cart before the horse, just as in Albert's case. The consolation "Now your father is watching you from heaven" – offered by the unfamiliar nun – is not yet appropriate, uttered before anyone has even wondered if Albert has understood what is going on. In fact, no one has paid him proper attention; no one has devoted time to him to explain what has actually happened (how the accident occurred, told in a way he can grasp). No one has helped him prepare for what is about to happen, the sequence of events that will follow (people will come to cry because they loved Daddy so much; then his dead body will be brought home, protected by a wooden box; then there will be candles, flowers, prayers, the priest, the church service, the procession, the burial at the cemetery and so on). This would to some extent enable the child to take things in and make sense of them. Above all, no one has helped him anticipate what will happen after the funeral: his mother's loneliness, his being the centre of attention at school, his longing to have his father back.

These would all be healthy steps in the right direction, giving some credibility to the consolation: "Your daddy is watching you from heaven." Otherwise, stereotyped, neatly pre-packaged consolations of this kind will only increase the child's sense of unease. If he had the means of expressing himself, he would say: "What is the point of consoling me if you haven't explained what has happened? What am I supposed to do with your consolations; for me they have no meaning? In consoling me you are using strange words: I've never heard you talk about heaven, so why mention it now? Who is heaven? Why has he taken my daddy away?"

Maybe the adults were still in their own "black hole"

Why then, when there is a bereavement, do adults fail to give a child adequate support, for instance by explaining what is going to happen? There are many reasons and they have deep roots. The first and most obvious is that everyone is focused on his or her own suffering, especially when it is unexpected, a bolt from the blue, as in the case of the death of Albert's father. It is amazing how the experience of suffering reveals a person's true qualities. If selflessness and the ability to engage with others are just something put on, suffering will reveal us for what we really are: our reaction will be little better than that of a "wounded animal" which goes away to lick its wounds.

If, on the other hand, the language of our heart is true, when suffering – even the most agonising suffering – comes, we will first be aware of the pain others are going through, engaging with them at the deepest level and so acting as a healing balm to all. In so blessed a situation – which cannot be improvised – Albert would have been received, prepared and supported; and (as we shall see) he would have had the experience of being able to give something to others. Above all, he would not have had to witness a murderous power struggle over the "right to suffer". It would seem that Albert's mother and her relatives went out of their way not to acknowledge Attilio's mother's suffering and vice versa. Death brings to light such "unfinished business", reveals it for what it is.

Maybe they themselves were not prepared for death

A second reason for the inadequacy of the support given to a child when a bereavement occurs is the taboo about death which has penetrated our culture. There is something paradoxical about this taboo: whereas the media feed us a diet of death and violence as we sit eating our fish and chips, death as a present experience has been outlawed, increasingly distanced from everyday experience.

We are no longer able to talk about death, or live with it. This explains why, in such circumstances, words like "heaven" and "hereafter" (there is a true story of a child who was found looking at a road map to find where this town might be) suddenly spring to our lips, dictated by embarrassment rather than forethought. Such words are heard even on the lips of atheists and agnostics, who have no other way of "justifying" death.

If children's first experience of death and loss is one that touches them in their deepest affections, it will be difficult for them to bear it. The weight of it will be both unexpected and frighteningly increased by their unfamiliarity with the whole subject. However, if in their extended family and among their friends at school they have heard death spoken of as a natural and inevitable part of human experience, they will be much better prepared to face it when it affects them more personally. Unfortunately, we are steeped in a culture which does not protect young people by educating them to accept death. When a death does occur, it is experienced as a sudden black hole, something contrary to all reasonable expectations. I know of a ninety-year-old man who – over a period of months and despite the fact that he was in good health – would cry out, "I don't want to die," and his relatives, the doctor and even the priest could find nothing better to say than: "Don't worry; you're not going to die." He was unwittingly emphasising the taboo that surrounds death in our society, inviting them all to participate in this tragic game. One reason why we are unable to prepare our young people for life is that we are no longer comfortable speaking about death.

Maybe they were too caught up in their own strategies

There is a third reason which causes people to overlook the needs of a child who is having to cope with the death of a loved one: the fact that – to stop themselves going to pieces – adults often superimpose their ways of dealing with bereavement on those of the child (the logic of which is often lost on adults). In this case, Albert's teachers were alarmed because Albert did not cry, did not cry out for his father and was not distressed in the way they expected. Their care and attention was praiseworthy; and it is true that anything is better than a laissez-faire kind of indifference. They might, however, have grasped the signals that he was working out his grief. They could have been more aware that – as we saw in Chapter Zero – children have resources of their own, ways of healing themselves, especially when the relationship with the person who has died has been an important one in their life. Contrary to expectation, an authentic relationship, though tragically cut off, enables the child to transform his or her grief by continuing to invest in the relationship, without having to give it up totally. On the other hand, a child who experiences the loss of a relatively undeveloped relationship, in which he or she was not particularly supported and protected, will be less inclined to fight for it. A withdrawal will be easier to achieve. The child will more easily surrender to the implicit prophecy: "In any case, they will all leave me." We shall return to the subject of the way adults project their suffering onto that of the child at a later stage.

Children are aware of the solidarity network around them

Now let us see how Albert worked through his grief and the possible dangers of the strategies he adopted.

First of all, he practised a certain restraint, not giving way to dramatic manifestations of grief, apart from the "normal" tears; it was as if he wanted to invest his energies elsewhere. Clearly, he was aware of being the centre of attention and, in particular, he sensed the solidarity of his friends at school. The completely natural way in which he received their little presents showed that he was living in the real world, that he knew exactly what it was all about. At the same time, the communication between him and his companions needed no verbal expression. Children are well aware of the value of substitute gestures; words would detract from their effectiveness in offering consolation. It is interesting that children give "real things" – things that are personal, used and loved. Had they consulted adults, the adults would have given inappropriate advice, such as "bringing money" to buy him a game or toy.

By giving something personal, his school friends were saying far more: "You do not need to be consoled or entertained or distracted from your grief; what you need is our presence." Pain is more bearable when we are not alone.

A child is inclined to live fully in the present

Where, then, was Albert investing his energies? Simple: in becoming his daddy. He is missing someone who will look in wonder at his exercise-book? Well, then, he can do it himself. He detaches himself for a moment from the work he was doing, looks at it as his father used to do and says: "Magnificent!" If you pay careful attention, you will notice that he is mimicking his father's gestures and even his expression. No harm in compensating a little for one's suffering! If we could learn from a child, we would comment: what is the point of making a fuss, getting distressed, calling for Daddy? These are negative efforts of the kind all too often made by adults. Albert is discovering a positive task for himself: actually embodying his father. He can allow himself to be like him and so feel the loss less violently. In this, he is encouraged by many positive factors he grasps from his environment: his daddy is a "man" like him; his mother evidently had a good relationship with his father, so "becoming Daddy" is not a risky operation that will devalue him in his mother's eyes. It would be far more serious if his mother forbade him to be like his father, if she disqualified him in the child's eyes, if she asked her boy to grow up in another way. This would tend to block his growth and result in a build-up of anger and fear.

Active and passive tasks

Albert, then, is permitted to be like his daddy. At this point, his mother could follow the line that the child is hinting at and entrust him with some "active tasks". Performing an active task in the context of grieving is a healthy strategy for coming to terms with it. For example, Albert's father used to bring in the firewood? OK, then, Albert can now do it in his stead. His father used to shave? "Wait till you're a bit older!" his mother might say with a smile. She needs to enter into the game and at the same time show him gently that she knows very well it is a game; that it is a good idea to be a daddy, but it is not magic, because sometimes he – like her – will really miss him. In other words, she can accept the child's "provisional arrangements" (his father has gone to another country) without having to appear to believe it totally and without weighing in with brutal facts.

The thing that a mother must absolutely not do (and unfortunately this often happens) is to give the child the passive task of consoling her: "Come here in the big bed with me, so we can keep each other company." I know of a sixteen-year-old boy who was still "obliged" to sleep with his mother. She would swear that he did not want to sleep in his own room; but it is a fair bet that if she asked him to do so, it was without much real urging! Giving a child the task of consoling his mother is to shut him in a cage, transform him into a custodian, a potential partner, a controller and saviour. One mother showed surprise when her eleven-year-old son questioned her insistently whenever she went out with a male friend, and this was five years after the death of her husband: "Did you kiss? Did you touch each other?" It was not that her son was "perverted", but she had transformed him into a custodian–partner–controller.

Environmental pollution

What then is the danger in a child working out his or her grief in the way Albert was doing? We can get a clue by reading between the lines of the story, which conceal a family "disaster". We do not need to go into the reasons, because – however serious the causes – they do not justify the breach that Albert's mother and relatives were determined to perpetuate between them and his father's family. The child effectively acts out the hostility, the malice, the alienation which he feels in the household; he refuses invitations from his paternal aunt and grandmother, tempting though they may be. And his mother approves of his doing so, exercising that strange ability adults have not to recognise their own influence in the actions of others. "How spontaneously perceptive my son is!" his mother might say. "He has understood, without being told, that his aunt and grandmother do not deserve to share in our grief. I haven't breathed a word to him! He refused their invitations on his own initiative!"

And we may well believe that his mother did not actually say anything; by her gestures, looks, anxiety and hostility she has already made what she thinks quite clear: if you dare to accept those invitations, it means you are not on my side. But there is something which makes it even worse: reading between the lines, it is clear that Albert's father had burned his bridges with his family or that they had burned their bridges with him. Therefore, since Albert is acting the part of Daddy, he feels to some extent constrained to assume his father's hostility towards his own relatives. Albert had heard the insults exchanged between his father and his aunt; he is well aware that his father did not get on with his own family. And so he is deprived of his "grandmother's pancakes" – in other words, a branch of the family deemed unworthy of their attention. As a result of the death of their son/brother, they would like to draw near again. Maybe his death has shown them how stupid their quarrels were. But Albert is a prisoner of the geography of hatred: if he draws near to his father's relatives, he will be drawing away from his mother and father, and vice versa. Who will tell this child that hostility, hatred and ostracism must not be allowed to have the last word? Who will tell him that death brings us to a fearful crossroads: either negative attitudes are consolidated and made definitive; or they can be melted away, opening up new horizons?

In the first case, there is a danger that the taint of hatred will perpetuate judgement and condemnation; in the second, there is the possibility of freedom and peace. Who will tell Albert that death can project a different light on what seemed irreparable?

Let me tell you a story ...

The town of Hereafter

There was once a little girl whom nobody could fool, because she had decided to get to the bottom of everything. Her name was Antonella and she had recently gone up into the juniors. She was very interested in history; but geography was her passion because they would look at the map of her town and identify the streets, the church, the school and even the blue ribbon of the little river which "bathed" it, as her teacher liked to say. A town bathed by a river was really rather an odd idea. But she – Anto to her friends – being very practical in her thinking, knew very well that the streets of her town were not bathed; you did not get your feet wet when you went for a walk! Then one day, when she heard that there had been flooding in Piemonte and the river Tanaro had overflowed, she understood that rivers really can bathe towns. For the time being, though, there was nothing to worry about: "her" river was little more than a bubbling brook you could look down on from the bridge at the entrance to the square.

Well, one day Anto-whom-no-one-could-fool heard some suspicious and very painful news: her grandfather had gone to Hereafter. She had heard it being whispered by someone as they sat around reciting the rosary among lighted candles.

And then, soon after, there was the funeral – a mysterious word that Anto thought of as being a greyish colour.

"My grandfather has gone to Hereafter," Anto repeated to herself. But if there was anyone who never went anywhere, it must have been her grandfather – apart from the little walks he went for with her, of course. When she came home from school, her mother was out, her father was out, her older brother was out. But her grandfather was there. He had kept her lunch warm; and sometimes he would add a nice titbit to the meal her mother had prepared – to the delight of Anto, who was a bit on the plump side. And grandfather Felix was always at home in the evening, too. Her father might well have gone out "on business" and sometimes even her mother would be out; her older brother, of course, was out every evening; but grandfather Felix was always there – even on Sundays.

"He's gone to Hereafter because he was old." This was the strange explanation she had heard from the lips of Aunt Theresa, who had come round to weep at that time; usually they never saw her.

"Well, then," thought Anto, "grandfather was already old before, so why had he chosen this moment to go to Hereafter? And without giving us any warning?"

And so, two days after the funeral, Anto got down to her research. She looked on her father's road maps; no luck. She even discovered that on the back there was an index of names, one after the other: names beginning with A, names beginning with B and so on. With great effort, because they were in small print, going down the list with her finger, Anto read all the names beginning with H; but there was no sign of Hereafter.

She then decided to go to the bridge and take a look at "the river that bathed the town", maybe hoping for inspiration. She followed it as far as her eye could see, to find out if by any chance the water flowed down to Hereafter. But all she could see were the banks descending gradually to the water's edge and the small vegetable gardens on either side, each with its lettuce patch. There were also a few big trees, putting their roots down into the water. No luck. She would have to resign herself to asking adults. Of course, Anto was not keen on asking questions, especially on certain subjects. Now that her mother would sometimes cry and the house seemed empty, too empty, Anto did not really want to ask questions at all.

"What is Hereafter like?" she began one evening at table. She had been craftily preparing her question for a long time, quite sure that they would not answer if she asked the direct question "Where is Hereafter?", maybe fearing that she would go to Hereafter to look for her grandfather.

She was quite amazed by the answers she received.

"People don't know what it is like ..." her mother began with a tear in her eye.

"Who on earth has been talking about such things with a child?" asked her father impatiently.

"In Hereafter, there is peace and happiness; people are always in good health ..."

"So why didn't grandfather take me with him?" asked Anto, but you could see she did not believe it. Grandfather would never have done something like that.

"Are you missing your grandfather, darling?" asked her mother, holding back a sob.

"What do you mean, missing him?" said her father seriously. "You've got to be reasonable: he was old and he died; it's as simple as that. You," he said, turning to his wife, "it's time you stopped your weeping and wailing. Can't you see you're upsetting the child? After all, he was over eighty ..."

Her mother looked daggers at her father and Anto understood it would be better not to insist.

It seemed strange to be asking non-family members where the town was that her grandfather had gone to, but Anto resigned herself to doing so. She must get to the bottom of it somehow.

"Florence, do you by any chance know where Hereafter is?" She addressed her friend in this way only on important occasions; normally she called her Flo.

"I don't know …"

"Didn't you have a grandfather, too?"

"Yes, but he's at the cemetery, or rather his coffin is," she added quickly.

Thus it was that Anto and Flo agreed to go to the cemetery, just the two of them, even though Flo explained that she had not known her grandfather very well, because he did not live with them.

When the two girls got to the cemetery, they had a good look round.

"Do you mean to say that all these people" – Anto pointed to the graves – "have gone to Hereafter?"

"I think so."

"Well, there must be loads of people who live at Hereafter!" said Anto in astonishment.

They wandered among the graves and stopped to read some of the names. When they came to grandfather Felix's grave, with the earth still newly turned, on seeing the photograph of her grandfather hanging from the temporary wooden cross, Anto burst into tears.

"Grandfather, why have you gone away?"

Next day, at school, it was the RE lesson. As a result of their long visit to the cemetery, Anto and Flo had not done their homework. The teacher was soon aware of the fact.

"I want to ask you a question," said Anto, looking her straight in the eye. "Where is the town of Hereafter?"

The teacher was taken aback; it was clear that she did not know whether to take the girl seriously or not.

"Her grandfather has died," interrupted Flo, because – as we all know – a friend is someone who will always come to your rescue when you are in danger.

"Oh, I didn't know!" the teacher answered promptly, approaching Anto with a tender look in her eyes. But why do teachers never know the most important things?

"You want to know ..." the teacher continued.

"Someone must be able to tell me where this town is!" interrupted Anto, relieved that at last someone was listening to her. "I've looked for it everywhere."

"But it isn't a town," said the teacher gently. And at the same time she beckoned the children to come and sit in a circle in front of her, as on special occasions.

"This rather strange word is used to show that life doesn't end here. When we are born, each of us has a place in this world. One ends up with a father with a beard; another with a father with a sawmill; another with a father who's a bit on the fat side; another with a father who's a doctor and so on ..." Mrs Cherry had the gift of putting things in an amusing way.

"And what about mothers?" the children asked at this point.

"I thought you'd ask me that!" said the teacher with a smile. "Because some children don't have a father, but every child has a place with its mother."

"Go on, then," said Anto-who-didn't-want-to-be-fooled.

"Well, this place is not final. No one stays here for ever. Your real place, your for-ever place, is somewhere else."

"In the town of Hereafter?" asked Anto brightly.

"It's a lovely place, but it's not to be found on any map. And no one can travel to it. There's not a motorbike powerful enough to take you there."

"Not even an aeroplane?"

"Not even a Ferrari?"

"How did my grandfather get there, then?"

By this time, Anto was bursting with curiosity, and she leaned heavily on the word "my"; it seemed as if her grandfather had become something of a hero.

"The door to this beautiful place is death."

"When a person becomes cold and can't move any more?"

"Yes, exactly. It's as if his body says: 'I've finished living here; my time is up; I am still alive, but somewhere else.'"

"And we can't go there?"

"Our turn will come," said the teacher, smiling.

"And so my grandfather's turn came. But why didn't he tell me?" asked Anto sadly.

"He didn't know himself, Antonella! No one knows the exact moment when they will pass through the door of death."

"But what do they do in that place?" replied Anto, who was always very practical.

"It is a very special place: the place where you go to be with God. For ever."

"But did my grandfather want to go there?" insisted Anto; meanwhile, her companions, who were listening very carefully, let her speak because it was clear she was hurting most.

"No, I'm sure he didn't want to go, especially because he would be leaving his little Antonella."

"I see," she sighed.

"But when your grandfather's turn came to pass through the door, he breathed a great sigh of relief ... At last, I've come home!"

"And what does he do with God all day long?" By this time Anto's heart was feeling lighter.

What a pity! The school bell rang. Bells can sometimes be very annoying.

Chapter Two

The danger of imprisoning a suffering child

Case study

Grace was as happy as could be. She had arranged to give a kite – a really big kite with brightly coloured wings – to her grandchildren: Martina, aged five, and Frank, aged three. A few days before, when she collected them from nursery school, she had told them to expect a surprise.

"I've got a surprise for you in the cupboard; on the first windy day, I'll get it out."

"Does it need wind, then?" asked Martina.

"Yes, definitely," said their grandmother. And she looked around as if she were expecting some signal or sign of agreement. She had let herself be persuaded to "abandon" them – as she herself put it – to go on a three-day parish outing. It was the kind of trip that she and her late husband, Charles, never missed; in the past, they had helped organise parish events. She had come back from the trip with the surprise she had mentioned, the thought of which seemed to make her very happy.

"Today's the day!" she cried, arriving an hour early at the children's nursery school.

The two of them tore off their aprons and let her help them on with their coats, vibrant with excitement in the pale March sunshine. Grandmother and Sister Nadia looked at each other and expressed what they both were thinking: "Poor things, they are entitled to a little happiness!"

Their grandmother, who always thought of everything, had brought a basket with a picnic tea. Their destination was the south-facing slope of a little hill; it was fifteen minutes' walk away and they would have to pass by the cemetery. When, on the last stage of the journey, their grandmother produced her surprise, the children were delighted. Even in its folded state, they could see that the kite would be majestic, a real queen of the skies. So they ran on ahead, in a hurry to reach the hilltop.

Amazingly, when they passed by the cemetery, they seemed quite oblivious of the fact, as if the kite were urging them on.

"Children!" shouted grandmother, struggling to catch up with them, "Aren't you going to stop and see Mummy?"

"Why?" asked Martina happily.

"What do you mean, 'why'? Let's go and visit her!"

"Later!" answered her little grandson.

"No, now. Surely you don't want to play with the kite before showing it to your mother!"

The children finally came to a halt and their grandmother caught up with them; she took them by the hand and led them to see their mother's grave.

The children had suddenly calmed down, as if reality had broken in. In the cemetery, in the part untouched by the sun, it was cold and damp. Martina remained unusually silent and their grandmother had to insist: "Let's say a prayer." Then she added: "Haven't you anything to say to your mother?"

"We've got a kite!" said Frank, and it was obvious that he was in a hurry to go and try it out. Martina, on the other hand, seemed to have lost her sparkle. She watched as they assembled the kite, said that it was lovely, held out her arm with the string attached and gazed at the soaring kite, which looked as if it might carry her away. There was a smile on her face, but sometimes a child's smile can be the quintessence of sadness.

"Poor girl! Not even a kite can take her mind off things," was their grandmother's comment when she handed the children over to her son-in-law.

Her second daughter's husband, a doctor, needed no convincing of the truth of his mother-in-law's words. He was doing all in his power to be a good father but feared that he would never be able to "fill the gap" left by their mother. Sometimes he was overtaken by a sense of unreality, asking himself: "Is it really true that Lucy has died?" A year had gone by – a long, wearisome year. He had reorganised his life to fit in with his children's needs, giving up his clinic at the hospital, which had given him far greater satisfaction, to do the work of a GP. Every morning, he took the children to nursery school with a devotion that would have moved a statue to tears. For the first few months, until Frank was three, he had left the boy at home with his grandmother, then had insisted on taking him to nursery school, so that he would have friends to play with. "You bathe him with tears," he said, forcing a smile, to his wife's mother. And she could only agree, unable as she was to "get over the tragedy". It was the height of irony: a young, energetic, happy daughter carried away in just three weeks by leukaemia – and a doctor's wife as well!

She had left two children who were truly delightful, to whom she was very strongly attached and to whom she had devoted all her attention. It was immediately clear that Frank, a cheerful blond little boy of two, would get over it; outward going and naturally playful, he would be able to forget his mother, at least to some extent. Martina, on the other hand, sweet little Martina, was bound to suffer more deeply. At the time of the bereavement, she was four years old and unusually sensitive for a child of her age. Tender and reflective, introspective though able to form strong attachments, Martina would have difficulty pulling through. The understanding between her and her mother had been too perfect; they resembled each other as the sucker at the base of a plant resembles its parent. Grace sometimes felt as if she had her little Lucy at home with her again, as when she was young and Charles was out at work. Sometimes she even called her by her daughter's name!

The suffering of this little girl, even a year after the tragedy, was painful to behold.

"I also miss Mummy very much," her father would say, hugging her to himself; and they would cry together. They would look at each other and know what the other was thinking; they would smile and know that they were doing it for each other, to banish their sadness. And Martina had extraordinarily sharp memories, which would surprise her father. She could remember the circumstances in which photographs of her mother had been taken, or correct her grandmother about a recipe because "Mummy didn't do it that way." Once she astonished her father. He had had a photograph of himself and his wife framed in silver; it had been taken in the mountains, the day they had first declared their love for each other.

"I wasn't born at that time!" she declared, having noticed the new photograph on her father's bedside table.

"And how do you know that?"

"Mummy once told me so when we were looking at that photograph."

Her father would dissolve into tears, on seeing his little girl so inconsolable, sure that no sacrifice was too much for her. When his mother-in-law brought the children home in the early evening – the moment he had finished his surgery, which he had organised in a separate part of the house – he would spend time playing with them, prepare the evening meal and entertain them until bed-time. Then he would bath them, get them ready for bed and, drawing on his deepest resources, tell them a bed-time story. By the time he finished, Frank was already fast asleep, while Martina was struggling to stay awake till the end.

"Tell me that Mummy will be back tomorrow."

"Mummy is watching you from heaven; I've told you so."

Then Martina would release her pent-up tears and he would take her gently in his arms, as if she were still a baby, and sing her sweet lullabies, while thinking: "Poor little thing; she'll never be able to forget." When at last Martina was overcome by sleep, he would lay her down as gently as the most skilled of mothers and notice that he was warm from holding her in his arms.

While continuing to live in her flat with its wealth of memories, the children's grandmother was quite young enough to run a second home. She spent her afternoons washing, ironing and tidying her "daughter's house", until the fondly awaited time came for her to pick the children up from nursery school. Not that they were unhappy there ... On the contrary, she recognised that the school was a blessing for the two "little orphans", as she referred to them in her own mind. Through them, she had been able to give a new meaning to her own life, and she would willingly have done more for her two little darlings and her son-in-law, who was very grateful but felt he must set a limit: "Take part in church activities, like you used to do," he would suggest. "You're still young!" But, for Grace, giving way to these urgings would also mean allowing him to seek consolation elsewhere ... And what if her grandchildren were then entrusted to goodness knows whom! Almost immediately after formulating a thought of this kind, she would regret it, reminding herself what a loyal son-in-law she had and, in her confusion, uttering a silent prayer: "Lord, Lord, I leave it all to you!"

Partly perhaps to overcome this hidden confusion, from which she was powerless to escape, Grace took refuge in the "cult" of her daughter's tomb – far more than she had in the case of her late husband. And, mindful of her role of educator, she also found that visits to the cemetery were a cure-all for Martina's troubles. Without a doubt, the child recovered her serenity in contemplating her mother's grave. Initially, the visits to the cemetery had been born of desperation, when Martina was crying her heart out.

"I want Mummy! I want Mummy! Mummy, come to your Martina! Why doesn't Mummy come?"

Her grandmother's heart had been bursting with grief. She, too, gave vent to her tears, trying to reach the child beyond the curtain of her despair.

"I can't live without my mummy!" And her grandmother could not but acknowledge the truth of her cry.

At such times, there was no way of distracting Martina; games, drawings, outings, sweets were all equally unavailing.

Then, one day, at the height of her "I wants", Martina said: "I want Mummy so that I can speak to her! Who else can I tell what I have done at school?"

It was as if Grace had seen a sudden flash of light. "Let's go to the cemetery!" she said. "There you can speak with your mother!" Almost with a sense of relief, she put her in the car and drove her to the cemetery.

The child, who had been there before, was so convinced by her grandmother's certainty that she began ("At last!" thought Grace) speaking over the tomb.

"Mummy, can you really hear me? Mummy, Cathy at nursery school has got a new Barbie doll. You remember that you bought me one?

Mummy, the sister said my drawing was the best of all. Do you know what I drew? It was a picture of you. I drew you with your shopping bag, so that you would come home, because the bag is heavy. Mummy, I know you can hear me!"

Of course, less than twenty-four hours later, Martina was given another Barbie for her collection, exactly the same as the one her friend had been given. Her father said solemnly: "It's a present from Mummy."

The conversations at the cemetery were soon the main topic of conversation between son-in-law and mother-in-law, because they were both convinced that what Martina said there revealed her true self, her wishes and fears.

There was no event in Martina's life, however small, that was not commented on at the cemetery, where the child continued her "private" conversations with her mother. This explains why, on the day of the kite-flying expedition, her grandmother had no doubt that they were duty bound to show the kite to her mother.

Suffering out of loyalty ...

Becoming involved in this (true) story will have triggered strong emotions in us: gratitude, on the one hand, for the web of love surrounding Martina; on the other, anger because we feel that she has been imprisoned in a cage, saddled with a life-long debt. How could this have happened? We sometimes come across adults, mothers themselves, who have been permanently trapped in this debilitating quicksand. I remember, for example, a forty-year-old woman having to cope with serious health problems afflicting her husband and a young daughter who was going off the rails. It was as if she was not really aware of these things; when she spoke about the "things that were going wrong" in her family, she seemed apathetic, almost indifferent. But when she happened to talk about her mother who had died when she was a child, she was a different woman. The statue came to life, her eyes filled with tears, her face was suffused with emotion. It was as if she were saying: "Having suffered so terrible a loss, nothing else can compare with it; there is nothing that can shake me." And she seemed convinced that her grief was "legitimate", if not praiseworthy, demonstrating her extreme sensitivity and filial piety. Not only had no one any right to distract her from her suffering, but everyone who came into contact with her had to acknowledge it. She was perched on the pedestal of her grief.

The striking thing about Martina's suffering is that she is totally given up to it, with no defence. She seems to have accepted it as her duty to be overcome by grief. There is no sign that she is working through it, allowing herself a respite, taking up active tasks (of the kind we talked about in Chapter Zero) in order to heal herself. Martina simply submits to it. In fact, at the very moment when, thanks to the new kite, she seems to allow herself the right to be a child again, she is unwisely called back by her grandmother. And at that point she seems to resign herself, becomes aware that she is obliged to suffer. If she did not suffer, she would be disloyal to her family system. Loyalty is the precious factor which binds, harmonises, keeps the different members of a family together. Martina knows – though she may not understand – that they all expect her to suffer the loss of her mother, for which there is no remedy. And so she suffers, being loyal and fully part of the system.

... to a family system organised around grief

But how could it have happened? How is it possible that a five-year-old child should surrender so completely to grief?

Let us examine two characteristics of a family system that involuntarily demands such loyalty from Martina.

The first characteristic of Martina's family is that it is organised around grief. Let me be quite clear about what I mean, lest I am accused of suggesting that a bereavement is something to be forgotten as quickly as possible, that people should harden their hearts and act as if nothing had happened. Of course, the father has acted rightly in reconsidering his work commitments and opening his surgery at hours which allow him to fulfil the dual father/mother role he now has to play. It is praiseworthy that he himself prepares the supper and puts his children to bed and does not want his relationship with them disturbed. The grandmother has done well in supporting her son-in-law. But what is obvious – behind this praiseworthy behaviour – is that every aspect of their lives turns around their grief. It is as if the mother, by her death, had fixed a new course of duty for each of them: the grandmother finds a new purpose in her life as a widow; the father is convinced that his grief and duty to his children should dispense with every other interest and commitment.

We might even say that there is something "convenient" about a death experienced in this way, because it requires each of them to withdraw into a niche, leaving no scope for adventure, the spontaneous and the unforeseen. In a system of this kind, the eldest child cannot but be loyal to the family grief; if she were not constantly thinking of her mother, she would be regarded as a monster.

The fact that the whole family is organised around its grief therefore creates a blockage, a sort of dam against life, and can never be a good thing, even though the intention of the system is to demonstrate devotion to the person who has died.

It must be said that some children are blocked in this way, even when the family is not so obviously organised around its grief as in Martina's case. Sometimes one person is effectively "delegated" to perform the task of custodian of the dead person, faithfully and obsessively reminding the rest of the family of him or her, while the others may seem detached or even intolerant of this attitude.

Of course, a child who observes and is increasingly sensitive to what the adults expect may be the one given the delegated task of preserving the dead person's memory. This is evident when the child persists in speaking in a put-on adult way, sacrifices his or her own interests and constantly refers everthing back to the family grief.

... to a family system where "everyone knows everything"

A second characteristic of family systems fixated on grief is that everyone already knows everything.

The fact of knowing in advance how someone else will react, what should be expected of them, will probably extend to every member of the family. The grandmother already knows (or maybe just ardently hopes) that her son-in-law will not "make a new life for himself", even though she encourages him to go out in the evenings.

The father already knows that his mother-in-law will always be ready to help – perhaps even too ready – and that he will have to set some limits, because "she is too fond of acting as grandmother/mother" or because "being a full-time grandmother is taking over her life".

But the interesting thing here is that they all already know everything regarding Martina: she is the most sensitive; she is the one who will suffer most. In fact, a large proportion of the system's energies are deployed in "protecting her" from an overload of grief, because they already know that "she will not be able to cope with it". Dealing with Martina's suffering (notice, I say "Martina's suffering" rather than Martina herself) is therefore a kind of tranquilliser for the whole family. Because it has become the centre of interest, it prescribes the attitude Martina will adopt, but the only ones who are consoled and relieved by it are the other members of the family.

It follows from this that the visits to the cemetery are a rather macabre way of exploring the child's grief, forcing her to suffer rather than setting her free. What intimacy can there be – as the grandmother naively believes – between a tomb and a child who knows perfectly well that her grandmother is listening? Are they not in fact teaching the child to adopt dishonest ways, so that even the desire for a Barbie doll is expressed perversely?

Of course, the other family members would be the first to express surprise if they were told they were imprisoning Martina in her suffering.

Her grandmother, for instance, would be hurt and would point to experience: "Martina is the one who cries and desperately begs for her mother. It's she who is inconsolable. We are doing all we can to console her, distract her and make her happy. Didn't I buy a kite for them, for example?"

Of course, their grandmother is acting in good faith. But the point – to stick to her example – is that she did not just buy a kite to give pleasure to two children. She bought the kite to comfort, cheer up and console her "poor little grandchildren". The two things are very different.

It is true of all of us that, when we already know everything about another person – or at least we know instinctively how they will react in a given circumstance – our expectations in fact influence the other person's behaviour.

Choosing to have faith in life

How, then, can Martina best be helped? It is easy to say that the family should not organise themselves around their grief, but this bereavement is hard to bear. Its impact upon their family life has been devastating; it was bound to shake them to the core, like an earthquake. What they need is to reorganise themselves, to find a new equilibrium.

It is not for us – nor even for the main actors in this drama – to say how long it will take, how many difficulties have to be overcome, how many steps forward and steps backward there will first have to be. But the important question is: what does this new equilibrium depend on? Why do they need to establish it? Why should they not allow themselves to be sucked into their grief as into a black hole?

When everything crumbles, we are forced to ask where we are going. The family – and therefore the irreplaceable world in which the child learns the elementary lessons about the meaning of life – is at a crossroads. Either they will take the direction of despair and become the victims of a cruel destiny (the more they turn in on themselves and try to stop the flow of life, the heavier the "defeat" will be); or they will grow in faith and trust: what has happened has a meaning, even though we now fight against accepting it. We can be sure that, if she breathes the air of confidence, Martina will pull through. In practical terms, if the father does not let himself be dominated by the depressing thought "I'll never be able to replace her; I'm just not up to it, whatever I do"; if the grandmother believes that her praiseworthy maternal impulses are a real blessing for the grandchildren; if she is confident about her maternal qualities; if they all let themselves believe that life will abundantly compensate Martina for what it has taken away ... then the decision to trust in life will be enough to help Martina make the leap from remaining in complicity with her grief to lifting her head and welcoming all the new "mothers" that life will certainly bring.

But the decision to trust is itself an act of faith. I am not talking about faith in visits to the cemetery, a general belief in a hereafter that has no influence on life here below. The faith required here, in its highest expression, is the confidence that Martina has in the *Abba* of Jesus – a Father/Mother who will not abandon her here and now. And fortunately, for Martina to be borne up, just a few crumbs of this kind of faith will do.

Let me tell you a story ...

What does grandfather do with God all day long?

Anto, the little girl who had recently lost her grandfather, was now quite clear that Hereafter is not a town or village. Her grandfather – as her teacher Mrs Cherry had told her – had returned home to a very special place with God.

The days went by and the question that had remained unanswered when the school bell rang – "What does grandfather do all day long with God?" – continued to exercise the little girl's mind. Meanwhile, it had been joined by another quite natural and related question: "What does he do all night?"

Flo, Anto herself and a little Indian friend who lived nearby could not shed any new light on this question.

The answer "At night, he sleeps" might have provided a solution. It was credible. Her grandfather used to sleep "when he was alive"; he snored so loudly that Anto could hear him from her bedroom.

"Goodness knows how the angels can get any sleep when they hear him snoring!" laughed Flo. "They are so light, they must be shaken by the noise!"

"But do angels sleep?" asked Ariela.

"No, angels don't sleep." Anto was quite sure of this.

"Well, then, your grandfather doesn't sleep either!" exclaimed Flo.

For some reason, the only dead person worthy of notice seemed to be Grandfather Felix. Maybe because his granddaughter's love for him, and her stubbornness in making enquiries, made him a known quantity, practically flesh and blood.

Anto accepted that her grandfather no longer snored and therefore did not disturb the angels.

"Let's ask the sister at Sunday school!" suggested Ariela.

The fact is that Anto never went to Sunday school at her local church. Her father and mother had never thought to send her.

"I'd like to go to Sunday school!" said Anto.

Her mother thought there would be no harm in it. But her father wanted to know: "How have you got it into your head to go to Sunday school?"

"My friends Flo and Ariela go."

"Why do you want to go?"

The words: "To learn about Hereafter" were on Anto's lips but she decided to fall back on another answer, which was also true: "Because I like being with my friends."

Her father decided that perhaps there was no harm in her wanting to be with her friends and said yes; her mother found out where and when she had to go, and who the teacher was.

So at last Anto was allowed to go to Sunday school. She did not know it was her grandfather who had been her guide in this. Had she conceived of the idea, she might have begun to understand "what grandfather does all day with God". Unfortunately, Anto was not able to raise her question straight away. All the members of her class were busy making a big poster about the life of Jesus. Flo and Ariela, too, seemed to have forgotten about it. Contrary to expectations, the sister had welcomed Anto with a smile and had not asked a lot of questions. Meanwhile, it was clear that the children were very happy to be together.

On the second occasion, Anto plucked up courage and, right at the beginning of the session, without looking straight at the sister (and in faltering speech, because she was embarrassed), came out with: "My grandad's gone and died. Now I want to know what he does all day with God. And all night."

The sister looked at her with a broad smile, scratched her cap and answered: "Thank you for asking so important a question. Shall we try and answer our new friend Anto's question? Who would like to begin?"

There was an immediate buzz of excitement and Anto felt rather annoyed because she had wanted the sister to give her an answer – a clear, precise and final answer.

"In heaven, people have a good time!" said a little blonde girl.

"Have you been there, then?" said the inevitable doubting Thomas.

"You never get stomach-ache and you can eat anything you like."

"If that's the case," observed Anto, "my grandfather could eat anything he liked when he was at home with us!"

"No," shouted another little girl, "in heaven people sing and dance and give one another kisses."

"Who do you get to kiss?" asked one young man, suddenly taking a lively interest.

"Great! You can kiss everyone?"

"My grandfather would never kiss everyone!" said Anto crossly.

"But what do we mean, 'with God'?" asked someone else.

At this point, the class quietened down and looked at the sister.

"With God," she answered very slowly, "means at home, in the heart of things, where everything is peace and love."

"So isn't heaven his home?"

"Heaven, too, but not behind the clouds!" said the sister, smiling. "It would be better to say at the highest, most beautiful, most lovely place in Creation, where all things have a meaning."

"Aren't we with God, too?"

"In a way, yes. But after death we are completely with God, so close that we are completely happy."

"So close we can touch him?" asked Flo, who had kept quiet until then.

"Yes, it's so beautiful, so lovely; let's die straight away," they said in a strange, spontaneous chorus.

"Just a minute!" laughed the sister. "To go to be with God, you need an invitation card. God, who is Lord of all things, sends a special invitation to each person. Because being with him is such a wonderful party that you have to be invited."

"The invitation is death," observed Anto. "My grandfather received his invitation, even though he was not expecting it," she said, almost as if to excuse him.

"That's right," said the sister, clapping her hands.

"Is he alone?" asked Ariela.

"No, there are lots and lots of people. My grandfather's there too," said Flo.

"So's my uncle. And Henry, who was killed in an accident."

"And my grandmother ..."

"And Mrs Louise, where I used to go and play ..."

The list went on and on.

"But do they all know one another?" asked Thomas.

"I'm sure they do," said Ariela, "don't they, Sister?"

"Ah, I see ..." said Anto.

"What do you see?" asked Flo.

"Now he knows them all, my grandfather has so many things to do!"

"And that's not all," said the sister, smiling. "Do you think he's forgotten you?"

"Oh, no," protested Anto, "I was his Anto! And he used to say to me: 'You'll always be in my heart!' And he must remember Mummy? And Daddy? And our relatives in Rome?"

"With God," said the sister solemnly, "no one is ever forgotten. Anto's grandfather looks down on and protects all the people he has loved. And everyone who is living."

"Let's hope he has a rest sometimes!" exclaimed Anto, who was beginning to get a bit worried.

> ***Things to talk about with your child***
> – Anto has continued to investigate the meaning of the words "being with God". What does she find out?
> – Is she satisfied now?
> – So can she forgive her grandfather for going away?
> – Won't she still miss him?

Chapter Three

Having to reconcile two mothers

Case study

Michael needed to have a heart-to-heart talk with his sister Ornella, who was deeply involved in the bringing up of his seven-year-old son, Luke. For some time now, Aunt Ornella had observed that her brother – previously so attached to the child, so attentive to his needs – was tending to neglect him. Some evenings he would go out with his new girlfriend and ask her to "do overtime", as he put it; he always felt bad about asking her to do him a favour.

He was well aware that, since his wife had died three years before, his sister had made great sacrifices for the child. Ornella had always been his "big sister", almost a second mother. He remembered how, when he was in the first year of primary school, she would sit him on her knee and help him with his homework, being all of seven years older than him. Even then, their real mother, who was always depressed, could not be relied upon. But fortunately there was Ornella, completely serene and obliging, whose presence they took for granted.

No one seemed to realise that, though apparently she had not experienced any great upsets, her adolescence and young adulthood had been spent in loneliness.

Everyone just found it *normal* that she should be around.

And then, when the accident had happened, and her young sister-in-law had burnt to death, imprisoned in a blazing car, everyone found it normal that she – auntie by definition – should take care of the "little orphan". In any case, her "little brother" – that is, Michael – was now more in need of looking after than ever before. Their other sister, who was just two years older than Michael and married with three children, was not a universal auntie like Ornella. Now approaching forty, Ornella was not showing any signs of wanting to take things easy; on the contrary.

One might almost have said that she had been rejuvenated by this family tragedy. She found it normal to look after her little nephew, in addition of course to caring for their mother, who was now permanently on medication, and doing her job at the textile factory, where they had agreed to let her work flexible hours. Luke was already at nursery school and, thanks to Aunt Ornella's dedication, had been able to attend regularly, since she had arranged things so that she could pick him up at 5 p.m. She would arrive, efficient and smiling after a six-mile journey in her Fiat Panda; would greet Luke as if she was always surprised and happy to see him; would take him home, play with him, tidy her brother's flat and get the evening meal ready. Then, when Michael arrived home on the dot at 7 p.m., she would set off again in her Panda and attend to her mother's supper. When Luke began primary school, everyone found it normal that he should be enrolled full time at the school in his aunt's village; his father took him to school in the morning, the school bus dropped him off at his grandmother's house in the afternoon, and Aunt Ornella would turn up shortly after to make him his tea, supervise his homework (if any was set) and play with him.

His dad had made considerable progress as a housekeeper: he knew how to heat up the supper, put his little son to bed and spend a "nice quiet evening", as he put it, while the child slept.

It had been Ornella – and only Ornella, if truth be told – who had been concerned that on Sundays too much of her brother's time was taken up with looking after the boy. She knew what an enthusiastic cyclist he was, and that his little bike rides with Luke were just a substitute for his youthful longing to take part in competitive events.

So she insisted that he get back in training and compete. In any case, she was there if needed. Michael had been very grateful, and Luke found it natural that Dad and Auntie were interchangeable.

Then had begun the question of "evening overtime". Nothing wrong with that. Ornella understood perfectly well that Michael needed to go out sometimes in the evening, in fact with a young girlfriend, another cycling enthusiast he had met at his training sessions.

Meanwhile, it had not escaped Ornella that nearly all the photographs of his "poor dead wife" had disappeared from Michael's room, except a smiling portrait of them on their wedding day. Luke's little bedroom, on the other hand, was still full of souvenirs of his mother that the boy had collected, with the help and encouragement of his father and Aunt Ornella. There were not only large numbers of photographs, hung in brightly coloured frames, stuck into countless albums, viewable as slides or on video, but also an entire section of his wardrobe that was "occupied by Mummy", as he put it. There was even the last piece of embroidery she had been working on, unfinished of course, almost as a reminder that her death had been sudden and violent, unfair. In addition, "talking about Mummy" was a feature of the times aunt and nephew spent alone together, particularly when they visited the cemetery. Luke in fact went to the cemetery twice over, because both father and aunt would take him there independently. For his part, he was convinced that his mother, whose presence he sensed in a surprising way, deserved his visits and anything else he could do for her: drawings, exercises and games that reminded him of her.

But recently Michael had been talking about her less often, and was showing some concern about his son's "cult of devotion" to his mother.

Ornella knew it was right that her brother should "make a new life for himself", and no one could expect him to remain a widower for the rest of his days. At the same time, brother and sister both understood that the real problem was "how Luke would react".

"He seems to have accepted my new girlfriend. She has tried coming round to my place some evenings and he seemed quite relaxed about it. That wasn't what I expected."

"But does he understand who she is?"

"Yes, I think so. He refers to her as 'your friend', and he is very pleased when she brings him a present."

"He also shows me the presents that Louise gives him, and he seems quite relaxed about it."

"He shows them to you, too?"

"Yes, and he calls her 'Daddy's friend'. It's strange but he doesn't seem jealous."

"Louise is a wonderful person, even though she is young. Everybody likes her; and she really likes Luke."

"He likes her?" Aunt Ornella felt a slight pang of alarm.

"Yes, very much. I asked her if the boy might come between us, but she just said he is a delightful child – thanks largely to you."

"Did she really say that?"

"Yes, I've told her about you and how you have helped us. In fact she says she would get you to help her, if you are willing."

"Help her to do what?"

"To be a mother. She says she would be very happy to take charge of the boy, just like a second mother."

"What do you mean? You're going to get married!"

"Yes, I think so."

"But isn't it a bit soon?"

"After three years …"

"Yes, you're right. Three years is a long time, and you are young … but does he know about it?"

"No, not yet. I wanted to talk with you first."

"But are you sure you want him to have two mothers? Couldn't you just have Louise as a friend?"

"I've thought about it, but I do not think it would be fair on her, on me, or on Luke. It's better that the three of us build a new family."

"And what about him? Have you thought of him? Will he have to forget his real mother and get to love this new one?"

"That's just what I am worried about, Ornella. It's becoming my main concern: I want to give him a mother who will love him, a new family to grow up in, but I'm afraid he won't accept her. I don't know who to talk to about it. I need help."

"That's quite obvious. We need to tread very cautiously. Don't say anything to Luke for the time being. First he needs to try and forget his mother."

"That's the thing I'm not sure about: does he really have to forget her?"

"To some extent, at least, Michael. Otherwise, how will he come to love his new mother?"

"Maybe you're right. So long as his memories of his mother are so vivid, how can he become attached to Louise?"

"I'll try to help you, Michael. We'll have to prepare the boy gradually."

And so, in Aunt Ornella's mind, the "poor little orphan" changed into a "poor little boy forced to change mothers", obliged to call a complete stranger "Mummy". She would have liked to cry out that she too, for that matter, might as well be called "Mummy". In fact, Luke had once tried to address her as mummy, but she had immediately put her hand over his mouth, telling him quite truthfully: "I'm your aunt and will always be your aunt. Your mummy will always be your mummy, even though she is dead." And now Luke was going to have to call someone else mummy! On the other hand, she, Ornella, was well aware that this would have to happen sooner or later and that she could not (and must not) try to prevent it. For too long she had been in the habit of thinking of everything and everybody – except herself.

So a "new battle" began, for the sake of and in agreement with her brother. They both left longer intervals between their visits to the cemetery, to the point where one day Luke asked: "But aren't we going to the cemetery any more?"

"Of course," said his aunt hurriedly, "we'll go to see if the grave is tidy. But it's not good to be too attached to people's graves. Your mummy is looking down on you from heaven."

At first Luke thought this was a bit strange, then he felt a sense of relief: his friends didn't often go to the cemetery, even though some of their relatives had died. Then, one day, his aunt thought the wardrobe needed a spring clean, and some of his souvenirs disappeared. And then the photograph albums, slides and videos were all put away in a big cardboard box. Luke seemed quite happy about it. Children are easily carried along on the tide of life, allowing memories to fade.

Then one day his father spoke to him, again in agreement with Aunt Ornella: "You know that Louise loves you very much, don't you?"

"Yes, of course."

"You know that when she comes round, she looks after you."

"Yes."

"Well, Louise is going to be your new mummy. We'll have a big party, all together, and the two of us will get married and you will be our child."

"When?" asked Luke, happy and full of curiosity.

"When you've finished your first year at primary school, in mid-summer, in August. And we'll all be together for ever."

It was like a miracle. Luke seemed to take the news well. He even told his maths teacher, whom he liked best at school.

"And what about you, Auntie Ornella, will you come and live with us?"

"No, darling, you know that I must stay at home with Grandma."

"And you'll always be my auntie? And you'll play with me? And help me to do my homework?"

"Yes, of course, I'll always be your auntie," said Ornella, who always behaved with the greatest sincerity. But Luke could not help noticing, though he said nothing, the look of sadness that had come over her face. Though unconcerned for herself, Ornella was really worried about how Luke would accept his new mother. And that was his father's worry, too.

Everything seemed to be going smoothly. But one day Luke noticed that his home was changing. The only room that stayed the same was his own little bedroom. His father's room was completely redecorated: they changed the colour scheme, the curtains and the furniture. And the photograph of his mother was put in a drawer. The kitchen fittings, too ("a bit old-fashioned," Louise had said), were completely dismantled and replaced. Even the bathroom was given a face-lift. His father seemed as happy as a sandboy. He was extremely busy with preparations for the wedding. Meanwhile, Louise began behaving as if the house were hers. When she addressed him, she no longer said: "May I …?" or "Would you please …?", "Can I help you with your bath?", "Would you like me to look at your homework?", "Would you like to see another cartoon?" Now it was: "It's time for bed" or "Show me your homework."

True, when she arrived she was always joyful and attentive towards him. She gave him even more presents and gestures of affection. As August approached, everyone looked on him with growing tenderness, especially Aunt Ornella.

But one evening he shut himself in the bathroom and refused to open the door, even when his father pleaded with him.

"I don't want another mummy. I've got one already."

"Yes," said Michael apprehensively, "that's true, but Louise loves you and wants to act as your mummy."

"No, definitely not. She'll never be my mummy."

"But you'll get used to it, really you will."

"No, never. I'll never get used to it."

"Come out now."

"No, I want my mummy!"

How do I relate to my father's wife?

We have the greatest sympathy for Luke: fate has robbed him of his mother and now wants to replace her with another, as if mothers were interchangeable. We also have sympathy for his father, who is abundantly justified in wanting to rebuild his life, partly for Luke's sake.

We also have a degree of sympathy for Aunt Ornella, who has behaved so truthfully but can now say with no satisfaction at all: "I told you that poor Luke would not be able to accept another mother!"

And so they have all made life impossible for one another, as if it were not difficult enough already.

What exactly is Luke being asked to do? He is being asked to accept another mother; in other words, to change mothers. To accept one, he has in fact to distance himself from the other; the two cannot co-exist. He senses this the moment Louise begins to assume the role of mother. Up go the barricades – barricades which become more and more insurmountable as he realises what they expect of him: that he give up one mother in order to accept another. Here, then, we have a conflict of loyalties in its most virulent form; he is expected to deny loyalty to the one and transfer it to the other. The tension mounts as he sees the signs of his original mother begin to disappear around him: photographs, landmarks, objects which belonged to his mother or were used by her. He perceives that they want him to abandon his primary loyalty. In fact, the more the house changes before his eyes, the more the reminders and traces of his mother are erased, the more he sees his father as "betraying" her for the sake of a new happiness (the rather starry-eyed happiness of people preparing to marry a second time) and the more he, Luke, is isolated in his loyalty to his mother. His loyalty becomes a dam resisting the flow of life. He will put up a long resistance before he finally surrenders. And even if he surrenders outwardly, agreeing to call his father's new wife "Mummy", the conflict may well continue inside him, smouldering under the ashes and breaking out in unforeseen ways, accompanied by a subtle and sometimes violent sense of guilt.

The right choice of terminology would of course help. It would help if Luke did not feel constrained to call the new arrival "Mummy". But there are few valid alternatives. The word "stepmother" has cruel connotations, while the term "godmother" – used in some churches to describe a woman who takes responsibility for the spiritual growth of a child of God – has been devalued and largely emptied of its power.

There remains the new wife's given name. Luke could simply call Louise "Louise", but in this case would he not be disappointing his new mother's expectations? But since when have the needs of a child – not in theory, but in concrete, everyday practice – been given precedence over those of an adult?

Acquiring new relatives without confusing existing ties

This is perhaps a good moment to digress on a practice we have observed in relation to fostering, when children are legitimately entrusted to another family for a limited period by the social services because the natural family is unable to care for them adequately. Ideally, of course, social services, foster family and natural parents (often the one remaining parent) will have come to an understanding that the arrangement is provisional and that, when the time is right, the children will be returned to their natural family. Undertaken as an emergency measure and regarded as the lesser of two evils, this is another of those situations in which a child is bound to suffer. But why make it worse by requiring children to call their foster parents "Mummy" and "Daddy", thus involving them in complex transfers of loyalty? Or should we encourage the children to refer to their foster parents in this way so that they fit in better with their new "brothers" and "sisters"? Children are not born *ex nihilo*. However compromised the bond may be, they have a bond of loyalty to their natural parents (maybe all the greater because it is threatened) and, when the time comes to go back to them, they will have to start using the old names again – Mummy and Daddy – for the people from whom they have been temporarily parted. Of course, the situation may be more complicated – if, for instance, the children go back to their natural family at weekends or perhaps once a month. Try putting yourself in the shoes of a foster child who is required to call both foster mother and natural mother "Mummy"! We have witnessed instances of children – entirely on their own initiative – making incredible efforts to bring order to this sort of chaos. Leti, for example, would call her foster mother "Monday's Mummy". Another foster child – Paula, aged six – one day asked her foster mother: "You'll always be my Mummy, won't you?" Warm-heartedly, the foster mother answered: "No, you have only one permanent mother and that's your Mummy Enrica." "Well then," answered Paula sagely, "you'll always be my auntie."

In a third, even more telling, instance, after eight-year-old Elisa had been returned to her natural family relatively successfully, she wanted to take her foster parents (who were visiting her) to her Sunday school class. But, while the foster parents were talking to her teacher, Elisa came to them in tears, saying: "My friends don't believe you are my ex-parents!" The reason for this upset was that, for children who have never been removed from their family, the idea that there might be "ex-parents" (Elisa's own invention) is fiercely resisted, implying as it does that parents may fail (i.e. become ex-parents). At the same time, their refusal to accept what Elisa told them shook her faith in her actual experience, because for her they really were ex-parents.

The social services, for their part, may be under the illusion that, once a child has been successfully returned to his or her natural family, foster parents can simply disappear from the scene. From a purely legal point of view, this is of course the case. But how can they expect that the foster parents will simply disappear from the emotional world of the child? In Elisa's case, they had lived together for four years – four precious years in which she had grown together with them and the other children in the family. Why should this be made to disappear? If a social network of "acquired/honorary relatives" were sustained beyond the period of its immediate utility, many conflicts of loyalty would be avoided. The new bonds established by fostering could be seen as extended family ties, whereby the foster child has acquired new aunts and uncles, cousins and so on.

A child is not an administrative problem that can be shuffled from one family to another. The child should not be asked to "suspend" the emotional tie which – since time immemorial in our culture – we have with those who have given us birth and whom we call "Mummy" and "Daddy" or, subsequently, the bond of gratitude and affection we establish with those who have loved us and shared in a stage of our growing up.

A conflict of loyalties

Let us return to Luke, who is involved in a far more radical conflict of loyalties, and look at things from his point of view. He is not a difficult child who refuses to face the facts. He understands perfectly what his closest relatives have in mind: they want him to change mothers. So he is fully entitled to protest: "I don't want another mummy." In other words, he is defending himself against a monstrous demand – the demand that he cancel his loyalty to his mother (as one might cancel a contract) and enter into a new relationship of loyalty. Forget one mother and accept another: a demand all the more amazing in that he has been brought up to conserve the memory of his mother almost as one might conserve things in a museum. And, in this, Aunt Ornella is heavily implicated. In a museum, everything must remain the same. The whole purpose of a museum is to bear witness to and preserve a past which would otherwise be forgotten. Normally, a museum is a place you visit, then leave again.

What you leave outside is life. But what we have to learn in this instance is that no one, whatever the bereavement, is permitted to set up a museum. A museum is a place of death, not life.

Rather than asking Luke to be the custodian of his mother's memory, he should be expected to discover that his memory of his mother will change and grow with him; and that this is not a betrayal but obedience to the law of life. It is a sure bet (reread the story in Chapter Zero) that Luke will find his own way of "keeping his mother with him" as he grows up. And this would be a good preparation for having another mother.

Unclear boundaries

Here we must consider the involuntary collusion of Aunt Ornella, who had taken over her little nephew's bereavement as if it belonged to her, as something in which she is competent. What this should teach us is that working through and coming to accept a bereavement means establishing boundaries. Otherwise, grief becomes invasive and will overrun boundaries that are already unclear, making itself permanent. Grief in fact helps to set boundaries – in a way it demands them – so that it does not become a permanent state but opens up new channels for life to flow in.

But, because of her own unhappy past, Aunt Ornella is already unskilled in setting boundaries. Where was the boundary limiting her role as substitute mother when she was a teenager? Where is the boundary between her and her brothers and sisters, particularly her youngest brother? Where is the boundary between the brother she once looked after and the father he has become (who now has a son of his own)? Where is the boundary between her role as aunt and her role as anxious/worried mother of "the little orphan"? And, most important of all, where is the boundary between her own life and the pressing needs of others?

It is clear that this lack of proper boundaries does not work in Luke's favour, even though Aunt Ornella's intentions are excellent and she is generous to the point of recognising that her brother "needs to make a new life for himself".

Grief, then, can help to show where our boundaries should be, if we allow it to. And this is a great gift.

Boundaries that cannot be crossed

The idea that loyalty to a mother who has died must inevitably be in conflict with loyalty to an "acquired" mother is again to do with boundaries. It often happens that attitudes to a child's upbringing that are unbalanced in one direction coexist with attitudes that are unbalanced in another. For instance, parents who are normally permissive in their behaviour may suddenly manifest attitudes that are extremely rigid. In the same way, Aunt Ornella, who is normally so careless of boundaries, inconsistently puts not just a boundary but an unbridgeable gulf between the mother who has died and the mother about to come into Luke's life. We all know of distressing situations in which the new habits the new mother forces the bereaved child to conform to are seen as wrongs done to the dead mother, expropriations of herself and her living memory. It is under this kind of stress that unprepared and fearful "new mothers" enter into competition with the former mother. "With her you did it that way? Well, now we'll do it differently!" – sometimes such statements can be a shout of victory, a contested area of territory seized with even greater force if the new mother suspects she is not loved as much as the other. And the one who suffers is the child, because he or she is the battlefield over which this war of suspicion is fought: "Why was he happy to do his homework with your first wife, but not with me?" And so the former mother can become a sort of rigid yardstick, a hidden controller, a real "skeleton in the cupboard".

Could there not be an alliance of mothers?

But who says that there should not be continuity between the mother who has died and her successor? Not in the sense that one must imitate the other because she had "succeeded" in being a good mother, or even less that she must discredit her as a bad mother, but in terms of life itself. Even among animals that live in packs, an orphaned cub is raised by another mother belonging to the pack. Life works in favour of continuity! This can be expressed in the form of a "mandate".

As long as our thinking is dominated by competitive instincts, and we spontaneously imagine that one mother would inevitably be in rivalry with another, we are bound either to expect a monstrous transfer of loyalty from the child, or that he or she will stick to the only loyalty that is really possible: loyalty to the mother who has died.

But if we can conceive of two mothers (or two fathers) as being allies, we can entertain the surprising, and joyful, idea of a mandate. In other words, the former mother can be seen as authorising the new mother to replace her to some extent, giving her legitimacy, and regarding her as a blessing for the child she has had to leave behind. This does away with the idea of a "real" mother (how unjustly we can apply this adjective) who has to be abandoned in favour of the new mother. In its place, we have the idea of a single "real" mother, who is a combination of the former mother and the new mother, since both are committed to implementing the laws of maternity.

Confirmation from the Word of God

Put in this way, it seems easy – too easy. But, if we are going to entertain the idea of a continuity of this kind, it is vital to consider our attitude to life after death. We realise of course that we have no direct knowledge of it and that it is quite pointless (or a distraction) to try and imagine it. Be in no doubt that all methods of contacting the other world (recordings of the voices of the dead, automatic writing and so on), albeit undertaken with a view to consolation and a degree of good faith, can only entangle us in our own mental contortions (those of the bereaved person or those of the people who take it upon themselves to "mediate" with the other world). They obscure our horizon and poison us, because none of us is permitted to make contact with a world that is totally different.

Of the people who debated with Jesus, the Sadducees were at least consistent in their views. They denied that there was an afterlife because, in considering the possibility in the light of the Law of Moses and of common sense, they came up against absolutely irreconcilable contradictions. If, for example, a husband died without leaving issue, his brother was required to marry his widow and raise up sons for him.

And what if – they craftily imagined – this were to happen seven times over? When the woman dies, and goes to heaven, whose wife will she be, having had no fewer than seven legitimate husbands? The Sadducees resolved the problem simply by denying that there was an afterlife. And one day they asked the teacher Jesus that very same question, to see how he would get round the problem.

The carpenter's son gave a masterly reply: it is absurd to think of the afterlife as a prolongation of this life. The experience of "life with the Father" is of a completely different order, quite beyond us to imagine. Our criteria, methods, arguments and crude points of view just do not apply.

Luke's father and aunt in fact imagine the afterlife as a prolongation of life here on earth. Therefore, to accept a new mother you have to forget the earlier one, transfer your loyalty from one to the other, love the new one and abandon the old. These are the ways of this world: substitutions, radical changes and returns to square one, with all their attendant rivalries, jealousies, taking of possession and disputes. The idea of abandoning one loyalty and replacing it with another applies in this context.

But what if the mother who has died looked on the world in a different way? Suppose her heart were not poisoned with jealousy and possessiveness and she desired nothing more than the good of her little Luke? What if she smiled on his father's new love and was leading Louise to be there alongside her child? Luke's mother is not jealous of Louise. On the contrary she is in Louise's heart, where she can continue to love her little one "in the flesh". Luke can accept his new mother because the heart of his former mother also beats in her. He does not need to give up one in order to love the other.

If Michael and Ornella can begin to think in this way, they will really be handing on a living faith and healing relationships within the family. They will be speaking this new language not as an educational strategy, not to sugar the pill for poor Luke, not as a means of persuasion. Far from it. In a way, they will be learning from him, from his own ability to heal himself (see the story in Chapter Zero), and gratefully acknowledging the rightness of his final statement: "I don't want another mummy." He is right. Without being aware of it, he is protecting himself with the bright shining idea that there is a Father who does not cancel out mothers and replace them as if they were spare parts for a car. Through the new mother, the former mother can continue to love her dear one "in the flesh". She still has arms to embrace him, tenderness to communicate to him, values to hand on to him. I said "in the flesh", but no one (not even Luke, unless someone suggests it to him) expects that the new mother will behave like the old, cook his risotto in the same way or tell him the same fairy stories. No. This would not be in accordance with the laws of life, which are against cloning! If we allow it, Luke will be enriched, because he will discover that there are different ways of being loved and ... loving.

Let me tell you a story ...

Seeing with your eyes closed

Naomi was quite sure Grandmother Valerie was dead. Dead as can be: still, rigid and cold to the touch. Her eyes were closed. If you spoke to her, she did not hear. If you called her, she did not look up. If you smiled at her, she did not respond – not even a twitch of the lips.

Naomi walked around her grandmother, who was not even called grandmother any more, but "catafalque". Grown-ups have strange words for things. Around the coffin were candles, flowers, strange smells and the lisping of a thousand prayers. Everyone said that Grandmother Valerie was very young to die, too young, not even seventy.

To Naomi, she seemed anything but young. When she came home from school, she deliberately showed grandmother her maths exercise-book, just to hear her say: "I'm blowed if I understand how they teach sums today!" And Naomi, with all the superiority of a first-year junior, would laugh at her grandmother's amazement.

And when she was doing her homework, she would say out loud, to amuse her: "Find in the set of fruit the sub-set of pears," or "Subtract the sub-set of pears to find out how many pieces of other fruit are left" and so on. Little Naomi had got to the point of chuckling to herself at school when she thought of how her grandmother would react to her latest instalment of modern maths homework. Now her grandmother was not laughing or showing outrage at the modern way of doing things; she was absolutely motionless.

And all around her people were crying.

Except for Naomi, who just wanted to get to the bottom of things.

Seeing that she had been wandering around the coffin all afternoon, her mother took her on her knee and said very softly: "Grandma is dead."

"I know," answered Naomi, without crying, yelling or banging her feet together to show she wanted her grandmother.

"Now she's looking down on us from heaven," whispered her mother, who was very worried by Naomi's unconcerned attitude.

"But how can she be looking at us if she's got her eyes closed?" burst out Naomi, almost amused, as if to let them know: "You can't fool me!"

Taken by surprise, her mother was at a loss as to how to answer her daughter.

"Has Grandma still got her eyes closed?" asked Naomi, when she saw that they were closing the coffin.

"Yes, of course," answered a grown-up cousin, completely surprised by the question.

Naomi felt slightly relieved; with her eyes closed, her grandmother would not see all the darkness there must be in the coffin.

The thought reassured her again when she saw the serious-looking men in black lower the coffin into the freshly dug grave at the cemetery.

But Naomi had no idea how her mother and other relatives could say that now her grandmother was able to see and understand everything. So Naomi found out that, when someone dies, children understand hardly anything and are left with many questions in their minds. What they usually do not realise is that adults find the same questions very, very difficult to answer, too.

By coincidence, at that time the RE teacher at school was talking about the Resurrection. Naomi was beginning to understand that, after his death, Jesus had risen again. His risen body is beautiful, perfect; he no longer needs to eat and drink. What is more, by his death and resurrection, Jesus has also opened the doors of heaven for us. We, too, will rise from the dead!

"Will my grandmother rise from the dead, too?" asked Naomi, who, whenever she thought of her grandmother now, felt tears come to her eyes.

"Definitely!" replied the teacher.

"And it doesn't matter whether she died young or old?"

"Not at all; in any case her resurrection body will be whole and perfect!" said the teacher with a smile.

"And will she be able to drive in heaven? Will she still need her driving licence?" enquired Naomi, who remembered when her grandmother would come and pick her up from school, always on time.

"That's something we don't know," said the teacher. "We don't know exactly what the future life will be like."

Naomi was not quite so happy about this answer. "And can she see there?"

"Of course she can see!"

"But how can she see if her eyes are closed?" replied Naomi. But just at that moment the bell rang, the class became restive and perhaps the teacher did not hear her question.

The result was that that afternoon Naomi paid a visit to the cemetery, which was only three hundred yards from their home. Moved by her request, her mother let her go, but as time went by she began to worry and went to fetch her. She saw her standing in front of the grave, hands behind her back, rapt in concentration.

"Come home now," she said gently.

"No, I'm waiting!" Naomi answered determinedly.

"What are you waiting for?"

"I'm waiting for her to rise from the dead!" declared Naomi.

"She won't be rising now!" said her mother, who again was caught off balance.

"Isn't it her turn? Does she have to queue up to rise from the dead, like when we go to the doctor's?"

"No, she doesn't have to queue up," said her mother, wanting to smile.

"So why doesn't she rise now, then?" said Naomi, unable to conceal her disappointment.

At this point, her mother realised that she was not up to answering Naomi's questions. And she understood something even more surprising: death gives rise to questions which no one, whether grown-up or child, can answer adequately.

However, Naomi's mother realised one other very important thing: we need to learn from children's questions and try to answer them as seriously as possible, even though, despite our best efforts, some questions will always remain unanswered.

And so, for Naomi's sake, her mother asked the parish priest to give her some "Bible study lessons". The priest was only too happy to do so and also invited some other fathers and mothers to come and find out what Jesus had said about death and the future life.

Some time later, her mother said to Naomi: "Thank you for asking me those questions; they were very useful to me and the other parents. Now I can answer you a bit better."

Naomi paid close attention and looked straight at her mother: "You see, God has invented a special place where you can see even with your eyes closed. It's a place where you see with your heart."

"Why?"

"Because you no longer need eyes. Someone who has died is with God and sees all things in him."

"How?"

"He goes on a special journey, for which you do not need a car or a driving licence. He enters into the life of God, who knows everything and loves everything; he created the heaven and the earth."

"And the more you enter into God, the more you understand everything?"

"That's right. He is light; with him, nothing is hidden, nothing is in darkness. So Grandmother Valerie sees us better now than she did before, because she knows better than before."

"Does she know everything I do?"

"The dead know the people they have loved much better than they did before, because in God everything is light."

"Does she know about sets and sub-sets?" asked Naomi curiously.

"I think so, though I don't know if they are of interest to people in the afterlife."

"Of course, they're of interest! She used to laugh when I did sets and sub-sets."

"Maybe you're right ... but we can't be absolutely sure about it."

"Of course, because we haven't made that journey into eternity yet."

"Journey into eternity, did you say?" asked her mother in amazement.

"That's what you said. God never ends. My RE teacher told me so, too."

"You're quite right."

"So, to make that journey, is she already risen or does she have to wait her turn?"

"She is already risen, because she is complete with God."

"And what about her body at the cemetery?"

"It has already begun to rise, I think," said her mother seriously, "though the Resurrection will not be complete until the end of time, when we shall all be in heaven."

"And when will the end of time be?"

"That's something we just don't know ..."

"And a good thing, too," said Naomi.

Things to talk about with your child

- Naomi found out something very special about her grandmother. What was it?
- Can we know, a bit at least, what it means to be with God?
- What does resurrection mean?

PART TWO

GROWING PAINS

In trying to sort out what is avoidable in a child's suffering, we must now examine another type of unhappiness, which is part and parcel of growing up. I am thinking of the various stages in a young person's becoming independent of his or her parents; family dramas, such as financial disaster, moving house or major decisions relating to the adoption of a child; and finally physical suffering, resulting from a passing illness or permanent invalidity.

In the stories of Henry, Sylvia and Francisco, we shall see – as you may already have guessed – that the avoidable component is more extensive. Living and growing means learning to bear suffering, accepting reality and finding the resources to cope. Therefore, we should not seek to overprotect children or overidentify with their sufferings. By doing so, we can make passing or partial problems permanent, cause children to think that they are unable to cope with their fate or make the past appear irreversible, so that it always touches on the present and becomes interchangeable with it. There is in fact much that can be avoided in sufferings of this kind.

In particular, we shall be looking for answers to some difficult questions. How important are the consequences of illness in the development of a child? How can we best help the child face up to them? Why is it that some children overcome such handicaps and others do not? Should one always tell a child the truth? And how does one go about it? Can we be sure the child has the resources to overcome the traumas, large and small, that are part of growing up? When is separation harmful or intolerable? How, in the case of adoption, for example, does one tackle the problems raised by other people's assumptions and attitudes?

Chapter Four

When suffering becomes a tyrant

Case study

For the nth time, his mother watched her eleven-year-old son Henry strap on his "wooden shoe", as he had immediately begun to call it at the age of six, when the "tragedy" had happened. And every time she saw him put on the artificial limb by himself (he was perfectly able to do it, though he rarely did), attach it to the mechanism worked by his knee, stand up again and try to move it, she was overcome with feelings of guilt – a life sentence for which there was no remission or appeal.

If only the imaginary court had said: "We sentence you to prison for twenty, thirty, forty years and then your crime will be paid for," it would have been a great relief. Instead, people were always saying to her: "It isn't your fault; stop tormenting yourself; some things cannot be avoided; accept it, accept it for his sake...", but she was unable to accept it. She should have looked after him better; she should have realised what was happening when he began limping and had to stop and rest after walking a short distance. Instead of chiding him for laziness, she should immediately have sounded the alarm. Perhaps the problem could have been nipped in the bud.

The paediatrician had reassured her, it was true. He had encouraged her to push him a bit harder. She had been only too happy to comply; in any case, she was fully occupied in the solicitor's office where she worked; she hadn't time to be endlessly dealing with the "whims" of a child. But in fact, poor little thing, he really was ill. She should have gone to another paediatrician, had more tests done. She should have ... When the paediatrician finally diagnosed a severe condition, the harm was already done. But he was only a paediatrician. What about her duty? Where was her maternal instinct? The truth is, her instinct had given her no peace, but how could she trust it when all conspired to make her take the line of least resistance, saying: "Don't worry; it'll go away by itself"?

"My foot's hurting," Henry had said, when he woke up from the anaesthetic.

"Your foot's hurting? It can't be…" she had whispered, overcome with anguish. The foot had been amputated. No one had had the courage to tell him so. They had all said: "You are going to have a serious operation, to get to the root of the problem," but no one had explained exactly what they were going to do to him. They all preferred to assume that he had understood. In fact, when he asked: "And afterwards, will I still be able to walk?" they had answered: "Yes, with an artificial limb," and he had seemed reassured.

Now, whose duty was it to tell him? Now that … And meanwhile he continued to complain: "Please, Mummy, call the doctor; my foot is hurting! Please, Mummy, have a look at it yourself!"

His mother tried to assuage her anguish by saying: "It's the wound, dearest. The pain will not last."

The clock seemed to stand still. At last it was 6 p.m. and Henry's father arrived. He found his wife completely demoralised and the child whimpering.

She took him aside and said: "Perhaps he will realise himself that his foot has gone?"

"He should have been told," her husband reproached her.

At that moment – she remembered with bitterness – the words had risen to her lips: "Tell him yourself," but she had immediately bitten them back, thinking: "No, not him. He's too insensitive. It needs tact. I know he'll make a mess of it." And, without a word, she turned her back on her husband and went back to the child's bedside.

"You know, Ree [the nickname she used in their more intimate moments], your foot was really ill … really rotten; to save your leg, they had to …"

Henry looked at her without speaking. His father stood there motionless.

No one came to her aid. The flood of tears she had been holding back burst out with sudden violence.

"Why are you crying like that?" Henry preferred not to understand.

"I'm sorry; there was nothing else they could do … They had to cut off …"

"They've cut my foot off?" burst out Henry.

"Yes."

"Cut my foot off? What have they done with it? And now my foot's missing?" yelled the child, tearing back the sheets to see for himself.

"Don't stand there like an idiot …" she shouted at her husband.

He came over to the bed, covered the child, caressed him. He was shaking.

"They'll put it back later, won't they, when they've repaired it?"

To the father, who was a mechanic, the question seemed quite reasonable and he started to reply: "Yes …"

"But what are you saying?" interrupted his wife. "The foot can't be replaced …"

"But the doctors say that there are artificial limbs which …" her husband said timidly.

"It won't be his foot, though!" she scolded him, as if he did not understand; as if, as usual, he was going for the easy way out … And so she went from one extreme to the other: from saying nothing to stark realism.

Henry's cries were now ringing in her ears: "Don't be stupid! It's not true! They'll give me my foot back!"

And she seethed with resentment towards her husband, who remained silent, incredibly silent.

She never knew that her husband, when he spent some time alone with Henry the following evening, had begun creating a fantasy world with him: "Your dad will earn lots of money and buy you the kind of car you can drive without pedals."

"And could I also race in Formula 1?"

"Why ever not? If you train hard enough."

"And could I also go skiing, take part in running races …"

"If you learn to manage with your artificial foot, you'll be as good as anyone!"

But Henry had never come to terms with it. And his mother felt increasingly enslaved by guilt. Every little problem was a reminder that she had failed as a mother (or that was the way she saw it).

"Mummy, my friends are having a race …"

"Mummy, my friends have picked the football team without letting me know …"

"Mummy, they've been teasing me, calling me 'peg-leg'."

"Mummy, why did it have to happen to me?"

"Mummy, what will I do when I grow up?"

What a blessing that there was Felicity, their elder daughter, full of kindness, sensitive and altruistic. At the time of the "tragedy", she was already thirteen years old and had a room of her own, but she agreed to sleep in her little brother's room. She became highly skilled in adjusting the artificial limb, to the point where they also took her to Henry's medical appointments because she understood how it worked better than they did.

In the evening, she was the one who helped him remove the artificial foot and put on his pyjamas, dismissing her mother with the words: "You go and get some rest; we'll manage."

Dear Felicity! She had become a real young woman, the best daughter any mother could wish for. And how patient she was! Not an afternoon went by without her helping Henry to do his homework and uncomplainingly bringing him anything he asked for. "He's my shadow," Felicity would say.

Gradually, she sacrificed all her independence to him. Her grammar school studies were very demanding, of course, but she had always achieved excellent results without having to try too hard, so she still had time to look after her brother. And her friends soon got the message; if they wanted to organise something, they had to accept that her shadow would be there too.

Henry always came along on the rare occasions when she accepted invitations. True, she had tried going out on her own some evenings, but on her return not only was Henry not asleep, not only had her mother had to lie down on the bed, but he greeted her with tears, appeals and insults: "Tell me you won't leave me again! You're cruel! You don't love me!"

His mother did not intervene to correct the "poor child", even though she would say that Felicity was doing far more than she really should. She did not insist that Felicity was entitled to a life of her own; she was simply very grateful to her and said so in as many words: "If I didn't have Felicity ..." and it was easy to guess how she might have finished the sentence: "... to make up for my useless husband!"

This tended to strengthen the alliance between the two women and the little tyrant could rest assured: if he failed to get something from one of them, he would get it from the other. If his father, who was less and less frequently at home because his engineering business was doing so well, should happen to say: "You give in to him too easily. I think you're spoiling him," he would find himself confronted by two tigresses ready to defend their cub:

"You don't understand how much he has to suffer."

"You're never at home."

"You never look after him."

Of course, when Henry tried the masterstroke of asking his father to take him to the workshop, they had cried out in unison: "You must be joking! It's dangerous! And anyway, what would a boy like him do in a workshop?"

The implication was that Henry ought to continue his academic studies, so that he could do a desk job. But at school he was a disaster. And he was so prickly and such a whiner that his former friends steered clear of him.

Only a few timid girls took an interest in him, letting him bully them around. So Henry withdrew increasingly into the society of women, learning little by little to tyrannise them. At the same time, he withdrew from the masculine world; and other boys, who regarded him as a "mummy's boy" – and so not worth bothering about – rejected him. Henry's world was increasingly a feminine one, dominated by mother figures – a world charged with piety and a sense of guilt. The boy was therefore poorly equipped for life and increasingly focused on his handicap. It became a bottomless pit from which he could draw a constant supply of demands and claims on others and an oppressive sense of dissatisfaction.

Every now and again, it is true, he wanted to escape from the feminine cocoon and, if his womenfolk had been able to see him at those times, they would have realised that he could manage quite well by himself. He could get around on his artificial foot with great agility, traded picture cards on equal terms with his friends, and in some games was more skilful than they were. But were he to arrange to go out in the afternoon and play in the square, alarm bells started ringing in the women's minds: "And what if ...?", "What if you can't get home afterwards?", "What if someone takes advantage of you?", "What if ... What if ...?", and eventually he resigned himself; he could not bear his mother's and Felicity's anxiety. In any case, he was not all that keen on going out; he didn't want to make the effort. The cocoon was suffocating, but wonderfully comforting.

One day, he overheard a conversation between his mother and Felicity: "It's true you can get to the university and back by public transport, but you would lose almost three hours each day travelling. And, in the first year, it's better to be there on the spot ..."

"So, what have you got in mind?"

"There's a friend of mine who rents a room in town ... I wouldn't mind, either ... from Monday to Friday."

"You've every right to, but ..."

"I know you're thinking of Henry. I'm thinking of that, too..."

"The only thing I'm wondering is if he'll be able to manage without you."

"I wonder about that, too ... He'll feel very alone in his little room."

"And what if he keeps making his usual complaints ... if he won't sleep, if he feels abandoned?"

"That's what I'm afraid of, too. He's still very young. I'd better give up the idea. I don't want him to lose the progress he has made."

"Generous as always ... you're right ... and then, it'll soon be time to change his appliance again and he'll have to learn to use it all over again ..."

Henry felt both a sense of triumph and a vague apprehension. At this point, he came out into the open: "You won't leave me, will you, Feli?"

"So, you've heard everything!" she said, pretending to be cross with him. "Don't worry; I've already made up my mind." And she gave him a kiss.

"See what a wonderful sister you've got," said his mother, with tears in her eyes.

Even the poisonous plant of guilt is a sign of love ... which needs to be brought to the light

We are all ready to say to this mother: "But you mustn't feel guilty!" Indeed, we are almost prepared to make her feel guilty for feeling guilty! We would readily come up with such frightening comments as: "But you're spoiling your son! Your son's real tragedy is not that he has lost a foot, but your own overprotectiveness; wrapping him in cotton wool and sacrificing your daughter is certainly not equipping him for life." Of course, these comments will do nothing to help the mother; on the contrary. Sadly, anything we say will be neutralised with the words: "That's true, but there's nothing I can do. It's beyond my power to do anything about it," and she will continue to shed tears, the source of which – in some cases – never seems to run dry.

Rather, we need to let her feel guilty. Otherwise, she would feel that she was insensitive and unable to accept her child's suffering.

Any mother who sees her child suffer is afflicted by a sense of guilt: she has been unable to protect and defend her child from harm. And yet, in every fibre of her being she feels that she was appointed for this role; feels that – if it depended on her – she would like to spare her child all pain, take every one of his or her sufferings on herself. She would like to transform herself into a kind of rubber to erase every one of the child's hurts. And she does not care a bit if – in others' eyes – she is being absurd in her self-blame (as Henry's mother is). It is all too easy for us to tell her that no one could realistically expect her to be more expert than a paediatrician, for example. Just by bringing him into the world, she has set herself up as the boundary between life and death, as his rock-bulwark-defence against the assaults of oblivion, meaninglessness and pain.

Let her feel that way. What sort of mother is she if she does not defend her child from harm? Let her be a mother in her own way. Otherwise, we shall be negating one of the child's most potent resources.

The greatest temptation that can assail a mother as she contemplates the suffering of her child is the thought: "He did not ask me to bring him into the world!" And therefore she sees it as her responsibility to defend her child from every hurt; provide "justification" for the fact that the child is alive. She devotes herself to keeping her child safe from every kind of evil; otherwise she does not feel she is a true mother. Therefore no sacrifice is too great; she is prepared to sacrifice her whole self.

But if the mother does not put up a brave fight to ward off this temptation, the child will probably lose the well-spring of the resource he or she most needs, the in-built capacity for self-healing.

The temptation is then revealed for what it is: the mother feels guilty for bringing the child into the world, because life has no meaning. Therefore, she must transform herself into a tragic goddess locked in a titanic but vain battle against the power of evil.

When religion adds to the sense of guilt

Allow me now to digress slightly concerning a readily available but highly destructive "solution". The "religious" mother (upheld in this attitude by large numbers of religious people who nurse the suspicion that God takes pleasure in making us suffer) points her finger at God and says: "He is the one who is sending you this hurt, this cross, this suffering; accept it from his hand and resign yourself to it." Somewhere, there is a god who sends us troubles and sufferings for mysterious reasons, such as (and I have heard this with my own ears) "balancing out the wickedness of sinners". "If you, my child, are suffering, it is a sure sign that someone is benefiting from your suffering, or it has been visited upon you to settle accounts; sin is paid for with suffering." But if he, the Lord of life, is the one doing the sending, how will Henry – and others undergoing similar trials – be able to believe it when people say: "God loves you; God wants you to be happy; God is on the side of joy"? A religion that sees God as the sender of suffering deserves to be protested against and overthrown. What a shame that many people (the younger generation especially) think that God himself has to be thrown down in order to do away with this kind of religion.

In God, the believer finds a friend, a companion, a close relative who shares in the hurt of every individual, and particularly in the hurt of those he loves most – little children. We have this on the authority of the only one qualified to speak to us of the Father's motives, his son Jesus. God is passionate about every human being, including those who suffer. He is near us and takes seriously the freedom he has given us. He is not an overprotective parent who, to keep us from suffering, takes away our freedom. He allows us to suffer the consequences (social and anthropological, as well as personal) of our endless refusals of his grace, our acts of self-sufficiency and egoism, our illusions of omnipotence.

Even a very small act of freedom on our part ("Yes, I acknowledge that our joy is your glory") is worth more than an endless round of suffering.

A magical god (magical in his omnipotence) might appear to be more attractive. But we have no choice but to take up our position on the mystery whereby he makes no concessions to our earthly condition, does not spare us suffering; and yet continues to be faithful to his original plan, calling us to live in joy with him.

Defending oneself against the temptation to feel guilty

A first line of defence against the temptation to feel guilty for having a child who must suffer is therefore to emphasise very strongly that the individual parent is not the giver of life; the one who willed the child's existence is the Lord of life. Life also allows us freedom in this respect. The child's *raison d'être* is not in the parent; if it were, his or her horizons would be very limited! Parents who feel guilty for bringing such a child into the world are doubly in error: first, for believing that they are the reason for (and purpose of) that life; secondly, for interpreting the future rigidly and negatively taking it for granted that: "The weight of the child's suffering will undoubtedly be greater than that of his or her joys and consolations."

There is also a second line of defence to which mothers such as Henry's, so exposed to the devastation of suffering, tend not to give due consideration: the possibility of sharing that suffering with the other parent – or rather, the idea that the other parent is of equal dignity and therefore that he or she is really suffering, too. Of course, Henry's mother would object that her husband is superficial, that he does not understand the seriousness of the tragedy, that he takes things lightly. But it is precisely this attitude – that it does not matter to the father so much as to the mother; that his suffering is less worthy, however it is expressed – that destroys the possibility of the second line of defence (which would have helped Henry). In the furnace of suffering, some mothers or fathers take on the role of "prima donna" and become tragically isolated. They do not realise that their isolation is due to their assuming for themselves an exclusive right to suffer. They somehow believe that their partner should express his or her grief in the same way as them, or they think they are qualified to assess the genuineness of the other's behaviour.

One of the most destructive aspects of suffering on behalf of a child – which can quite easily destroy a marriage – is the conviction that only I am suffering so badly, only I really understand what the child is going through: "My partner is not hurting in the same way as I am." Why does Henry's mother not give credit to the various ways in which his father participates in the child's suffering? Suffering loses much of its power if it is rooted in the couple. When this is the case, communication between husband and wife overcomes the barriers set up by the selfish ego and suffering is expressed in terms of "we". There are couples who emerge strengthened from the experience of suffering on behalf of a child – and this is of course a source of strength for the child.

How to protect the child ...

At the same time, a child will be able to appreciate the positive side of suffering only if the parents see and deal with him or her as a person who is capable of overcoming it; an individual who, however hard the road may be, will know times of joy and a sense of achievement. Henry could live with an artificial foot, not denying the reality of the limitations it imposes but nevertheless feeling that other possibilities are open to him.

Using one's suffering to subject, blackmail and nail down others is a losing strategy, even though Henry may be able to snatch momentary victories, such as keeping his elder sister at home. The guilty feelings of his mother are unhelpful hooks on which he hangs his endless desires to get his own way. But, in so doing, he is becoming the victim of his sufferings, his limitations, his handicap. It is amazing how this can happen.

... and not rope others in

Since Henry's mother cannot live with her guilty feelings (it would be better to say her error or limitations), she has roped her daughter into her all-consuming, overprotective cosseting, which knows no bounds where "poor" Henry is concerned. Up to a certain point, Felicity may emerge strengthened by the experience, because a mother's admiration, esteem and trust are priceless assets. Unfortunately, though, there is a danger that she will feel she is loved only if she undertakes to serve her younger brother. Her horizon of development is likely to be restricted by the conviction that she is in the "second division" compared with her brother, and her being "good" (a very simplistic notion of good behaviour!) will become the condition of her existence. Everyone – and not just Felicity – will pay a high price for this good behaviour.

But it is also clear that the alliance between mother and daughter expresses a need (unconscious, of course!) of the child's suffering as the guarantee of their being together, supporting each other, resisting any possibility of separation. They uphold each other in the face of loneliness, meaninglessness, anguish. As long as they continue to "fill the gap", they have a task which keeps them from having to cross the abyss.

Basically, whenever a family situation is organised around a handicap, with all expressions of family life structured in relation to a suffering which demands everyone's constant attention (each system will have its own word for it, be it "tragedy", "misfortune" or "affliction"), it will probably have its "convenient" side. In other words, it will serve as an excuse for ignoring other sufferings, which may be even worse. If a sister feels she must give up the idea of going away to university so that her brother does not have to sleep alone at night, it probably means she is afraid of separation or of losing her mother's esteem. Or maybe she is afraid of discovering that she is not loved if she leaves her mother to cope alone. In this case, the younger brother in need of care and attention is a good excuse for not facing up to reality.

Who was there to help this family?

As we have seen, Henry has his reasons for behaving as he does, and he reaps certain advantages from his behaviour, but there are even more important things he is missing out on: his father's workshop, games on equal terms with his peers, the little misdemeanours he might get up to on his own (these, too, are an important part of growing up) and the tasks and challenges he might set himself. For Henry, this all seems to be forbidden territory.

But why does he give it all up so easily? Why does he not loudly demand his independence? As we have already noted, the adult world around him is full of negative prophecies: you will not be able to cope; your handicap disqualifies you from leading a full life. But it is also related to another factor, which it is now time to mention.

People often wonder if it is right to tell a child the whole truth about an event such as a surgical operation which cannot be avoided. The sad fact is that Henry was not prepared for it. The information he was given was vague and the message did not get across to him.

There is no substitute for parents in such circumstances, but hospital staff and psychiatric social workers do have a duty to prepare parents for this sort of task. Fortunately, nowadays healthcare professionals – at least in some hospitals – seem to be more attentive to the need to support both the parents and children concerned (for instance, parents are encouraged to stay in hospital with their child; play and learning areas have been created for long-stay patients; and child patients are encouraged to form friendships with other children on the ward). It is therefore now a good deal easier to tell a child the truth in good time, but of course just providing information is not enough. A child needs to be helped to understand what is going to happen, and he or she must be allowed to express feelings of fear and anguish. The child needs to be told: "Such and such a thing is going to happen to you, but it will not be for ever." Giving a context to the suffering the child has to undergo (explaining the timetable: first, this is going to happen ... then ...) is a way of arousing his or her inner resources, which are so vital if the child is to live a worthwhile life. Henry was robbed of this kind of preparation. But who helped his mother and father to face up to the suffering their child would have to undergo?

Let me tell you a story ...
A clever trick
Barbara opened her eyes and found herself in a strange, strange world: tubes, wires, machines, strange noises and – amazingly – her mother in a green overall, face mask and gloves. She quickly closed her eyes, because the dream was so unusual, but opened them again almost immediately, because she had been struck by her mother's eyes – eyes that were wide open with happiness. Her mother's eyes

were still there, still wide open, but her happiness concealed a small question mark: "Barbara ... darling ... my treasure ..."

"Hello, Mummy."

"Oh, thank you, Lord, you're alive! How are you? Are you OK? Is there anything you want; are you hurting anywhere; how do you feel? Now you can see me, you can speak to me, give me a sign ..." Nothing could stop the flow of words. It was as if her mother were afraid Barbara might disappear again into who knows what hidden world.

Barbara forced herself to smile, even though she found it tiring. Meanwhile, her mother had rung all the bells she could get her hands on and repeated to every nurse who came in: "Call my husband! He should be here! The Lord is here! He has answered my prayer!" In her wild excitement, she was causing such confusion that a doctor who had just come in was obliged to say: "Madam, please calm down, or I shall have to ask you to leave."

Then the doctor leaned over Barbara, carefully touching her and arranging the wires, as if to make sure she was still there and intact.

"Where am I?" Barbara finally stammered, making a great effort to get the words out in the right order.

"You're in hospital, darling," said her mother excitedly, "but you are being well looked after."

"You had an accident," explained the doctor. "You were hit by a car as you were crossing the road and you – clever girl – just closed your eyes tight so as not to see what happened next. Now, though, we're very pleased you have opened them again," he continued confidentially, giving her cheek a little pinch.

"I closed my eyes and didn't feel anything?" asked Barbara, who was now completely awake.

"Yes, and you went into a nice deep sleep. That gave us the chance to attach all these wires to you and transform you into something like a Martian," answered the doctor, who obviously enjoyed a joke.

"And have I been asleep for a very long time?"

"Long enough to have a whole week off school!" he replied.

"They all came to see you, from the other side of the glass screen, your friends and teachers ..." added her mother, with tears in her eyes.

Suddenly Barbara felt very tired and closed her eyes again. The doctor checked the readings on the various machines, touched her cheek, warned her mother to keep calm and left the room.

But Barbara could hear everything, even though her eyes were closed.

"She's come out of the coma, you can rest assured," the nurse said to her mother.

"And what if she lapses back into a coma?" asked her mother with growing agitation.

"No, that won't happen; you can see that all the readings are normal."

So Barbara learned the meaning of the word "coma", understood it instinctively. She had a vague memory of having come across the word at school, in a story, or perhaps on the television news. Now, though, the meaning was clear: it was the long, deep sleep she had withdrawn into so as not to feel or see anything – a temporary escape from life.

The doctor was right; it was a clever trick. The only thing she could see clearly was that her mother had suffered greatly.

Suddenly, her father came in, still in his work clothes. He slipped into the room confidently, boldly, as if he were ten years younger. He had received the news that Barbara had come out of her coma at the factory, and it had been joyful music to everyone's ears, workmates and foreman alike. They all said: "Go straight away, Albert. It's a moment not to be lost."

So, here he was, almost embarrassed to be there. Barbara, despite the fact that her eyes were closed, could "see" him from her mother's reactions.

"She's come out of it; she's come out of it! What a blessing!" she was laughing and crying as she clung to his shoulder.

"And has she said anything?"

"Yes, she asked where she was. Really, she has been miles away."

"Let me try calling her …"

"No, steady on! Let her open her eyes when she wants to; we mustn't tire her out; we mustn't …"

But, at that moment, Barbara opened her eyes and looked into her father's.

"Oh, just as well," he said, "or else I'd have thought you had something against me!" Like the doctor, he seemed able to make a joke of it.

Barbara's eyelids closed again, but she remained very aware of what was going on. They were making plans for the future. Barbara's heart beat faster. Never had she realised, in all her ten years in the world, that she was so precious to her mother and father. "Who knows?" she thought later when remembering those moments. "Maybe the occasional coma would not be a bad thing for many children!"

Her mother was having pleasant thoughts of a big glass bell in which she could keep her daughter, to protect her in future, not just from accidents but from every little draught of wind. Poor Mummy; you have to try and understand her; she was the one who had kept watch at Barbara's bedside for seven days and seven nights, almost without a break. How had she done it? Now nothing would be allowed to take her daughter away again: "We'll just have to write off this year's schooling …" she whispered.

"What do you mean? It's only Easter! Is that what the doctors told you?"

"No, no, they haven't said anything … it's just that, with everything that has happened …"

"Hang on a minute. When she's better, she's better, isn't she? Didn't the doctors tell us that if she came out of the coma all right, there wouldn't be any further consequences?"

"That's what they said, yes. But we'll just have to see …"

"Exactly. Let's leave the decisions to them. What you need now is a bit of rest …"

"Definitely not … I'm staying here …"

"… glued to the spot! And since when have you been irreplaceable?"

"You wouldn't want my Barbara to …"

"So it's 'my' Barbara now, is it? And where do I come into it?"

"You're her father, I know. I don't want to take her away from you …"

"She'll be needing me, too," he intimated proudly.

"Yes, but you've got your work to do."

"I've been thinking that Barbara might cure me of my overtimeitis ..."

"What's that you say?" his wife asked incredulously.

"I said that I'll be home every day at five-thirty, on the dot."

"But didn't you tell me it was impossible?"

"I've thought about it. I don't want a situation where, because I am working so hard, the children grow up without me around and I hardly know them."

"You really have been thinking," his wife answered with an infinitely tender laugh.

"But let's get one thing straight," he said seriously, "we're not going to wrap her in cotton wool; we must let her lead a normal life."

"So normal that we'll all be together on Saturdays and Sundays, and you'll take us out somewhere?"

"Now don't go building castles in the air!" he laughed, but he was obviously pleased by his wife's reaction.

At this point, Barbara lapsed into a deep, healing sleep.

Things to talk about with your child

- In what sense was Barbara's coma a "clever trick"?
- What did Barbara come to understand as a result of her accident?
- How will she be able to face life now?

Chapter Five

When children have to "nurse" their parents

Case study

The bell rings for break and groups of children rush out into the school playground, heeding the call of freedom. It is a warm October morning and the sun has lit up the playground, as if in preparation for the invasion of little feet impatient to get out of the classroom. The children chase one another, shout, join hands and fly apart as they play ever-changing games, the only aim of which seems to be to satisfy their need for movement. Almost everyone has something to eat, pulling from their pockets croissants, biscuits or chocolate bars. The odd child who is not eating keeps an eye on the school gate and, as soon as mother or granny approaches, charges over, reaches through the bars and, with a hurried greeting, grabs the proffered sandwich or apple, then returns to the game. The child barely answers the parental enquiry "How are you?", responding with a vague "Fine!" There is no time to lose. There is a more pressing need to play, make a noise, exercise vocal cords as well as little legs.

A few grannies and child-minders are standing at the gate with their prams or pushchairs. The babies they are minding are conscious of the joyful hubbub of the playground and clap their hands with pleasure. It is an exciting spectacle, far more interesting than a television cartoon; children just one or two years old know it instinctively.

At this moment, a mother arrives. "Sylvia!" she calls, searching for her daughter among the scurrying children: "Sylvia!" From her expression, it is clear she is not at peace.

Sylvia detaches herself from a knot of shouting girls who have been chasing one another around the playground and goes over to her mother, the spring suddenly gone from her step: "Hello, Mummy."

"Have you eaten your biscuits?" she asks, surveying every detail of the girl's face and slim body with anxious eyes.

"Yes."

"Are you sure? Did you eat them all?"

"Yes."

"And how has school been?"

"Fine."

"Did you cry?"

"No."

Her mother continues to watch the girl, as if something has escaped her. Sylvia, now detached from her friends, who are going on with their game, leans against the gate, adopting a rather passive attitude, as if she is not very interested. Her mother manages to take her by the hand and scrutinises her.

At that moment, the bell rings. From the top of the steps leading up to the building, a teacher claps her hands to get the attention of the children still engrossed in their play. All the teachers are there, each waiting to gather his or her own group of children. Even on the faces of some of the teachers it is possible to read a reluctance to abandon the warm October sunshine. In a few seconds, the children line up, class by class.

"Go on, then," says Sylvia's mother, moving away from the gate.

Sylvia seems slow and uncertain. For a moment, she rubs herself against the gate, reluctant to go.

"Go on now!" says her mother encouragingly, with a farewell wave of her hand. "Be a good girl."

If you did not know that in a short while Sylvia would be back home again, you might think that the two were anticipating a long period of separation.

"Sylvia, we're just waiting for you!" shouts her teacher. At last, the girl, who has taken a few steps as if to accompany her mother, tears herself away from the gate and rejoins the group.

"Is it her first year?" asks a grandmother, who is looking after a small child, jumping up and down in his pushchair.

"Yes, it's her first year. Sylvia is not used to being away from me," adds her mother, as if to justify her being there.

"Before you arrived, she was playing with all the others."

"Yes, I know. But in the morning she is so reluctant to get up … She never wants her breakfast … She's like a snail. It makes me feel so bad. So during break I come to see if she's eaten her biscuits. Anyway, I live very near here."

"I saw you get out of the car …"

"It's just three minutes in the car. No distance at all. I haven't missed a morning since Sylvia has been going to school."

"And do you come and pick her up later?"

"Of course! There is a school bus, but it takes a good twenty minutes to get her home. I can be here in a flash."

"We're still having some lovely days."

"Thank goodness! That means I can come and watch her play. When it's cold or wet, I can't go inside the building!"

At lunchtime, Sylvia almost always eats what her mother has prepared for her, even though she does not seem very keen on her food. But the thing that really bothers her mother is that Sylvia is not talkative. She never has been, it is true, not even when she was at nursery school – which she attended, though not very regularly. Now, though, she says hardly anything, while her mother would like to take an interest in everything she does at school, be involved in her life, know all about it: "Well, what did you do today?"

"We drew."

"And did you do a nice drawing?"

"Yes."

"And what did you do after that?"

"We had to look for letters in words written on the blackboard."

"And did you get them right?"

"Yes."

"That's good, Sylvia. Then what did you do?"

Her mother continues to ask questions, not realising that she is conducting an interrogation. Sylvia answers as if she had been taken captive. Her monosyllabic responses irritate her mother; she feels envious of her friends, who know all about what their children do at school. Why do other children, especially the girls, tell their mothers everything, while getting information from Sylvia is like squeezing water from a stone? Because she is not happy at school? Because she feels sad? Perhaps they do not treat her properly? She will have to try and find out ... If only she were one of those mothers whose daughters are so chatty that they even know how many times the teacher coughed! It is obvious that if her Sylvia is behaving like this, there must be something wrong.

A vicious circle

Sylvia's mother would be quite amazed if she realised that Sylvia is in fact "nursing" her, taking care of her and trying – quite unconsciously – to ensure that her mother does not suffer too much from their separation. Children are generous by nature. If they sense a need in the adult who is closest to them, they try to meet it as best they can. How would her mother react if Sylvia were to say: "Give me a bit of space, Mum; I'm getting on very well here; I don't need you"? Sylvia knows instinctively what her mother would feel (even though she might not say it in so many words): "Well then, what do I mean to you, if you can get on perfectly well without me?"

To an outsider, it is obvious: if all that Sylvia's mother wants is to be reassured that her child is happy at school, she need only observe her, without being seen, while Sylvia is playing. She would then be left in no doubt that her child is coping among her peers, even if she is not cut out to be a leader of men (or girls). Why then does she need to call Sylvia over? To make her aware of her presence? To reassure her? Sylvia therefore detaches herself from the group and tries to reassure her mother: "You see, I'm not really happy without you", "You see I need you." Then it is her mother's turn to reassure Sylvia that she is her prime concern, and Sylvia is then bound to reassure her mother in turn: "There is nothing specially interesting about school." A vicious circle has been established.

This unfortunate circle of mutual reassurance will probably trigger a whole series of circles, like a stone thrown into a pond. The anxiety of the investigating, interrogating mother is countered by her daughter, who tries to protect herself from her mother's anxiety by answering in monosyllables. The mother's more and more urgent attempts to learn about her daughter's life at school because she suspects that something is wrong are met by increasing reticence on the part of her daughter. And so it goes on. Then there is the vicious circle of envy: the child cannot understand why she cannot have her own private space like her friends, who are allowed to spend their break without maternal intrusions. So she draws into her shell and communicates as little as possible. The less she is forthcoming, the more her mother envies her friends who know all about their children's doings at school.

When children are obliged to console their parents

Here, then, we have a six-year-old girl who is "obliged" to console her mother for her being separated from her. There is nothing wrong in this, up to a certain point. All children take steps to reassure, console and be close to their parents. It is even better if, as children grow, they begin to do so consciously. Many adolescents would do well to try and put themselves in their parents' shoes occasionally, making at least a crack in the great wall of their selfishness. It would be a salutary lesson, especially since they have the mental capacity to do so. They might discover, for instance, that they could come home at the time agreed, or tidy their room, as a way of taking care of their parents.

Sylvia, then, takes care of her mother – albeit unconsciously – reassuring her mother of her importance in her life, letting her know that she is her sun and centre of gravity; that she cannot be really happy when she is away from her.

But why should it be necessary to reassure her mother? What is going on that the mother finds so alarming? It is that the bogey of separation has appeared on the horizon. She is facing one of the many dramas of separation that characterise human life. The issue of separation does not first arise when sons or daughters leave home to establish their own family, taking a responsible, mature decision. Sons or daughters can make that sort of decision only because they have already become expert in the art of walking away. They have proved over and over again that one can walk away while continuing to love, without destroying the other person. But to arrive at that point, they have had to explore healthy, appropriate, creative ways of becoming their own person.

If Sylvia's mother could find a way of saying to her (not, of course, in words, which would sound artificial, but by her behaviour): "There is nothing wrong with your having some private areas in your life which are closed to me," Sylvia would probably feel much freer and would show her mother that she could cope with life adequately – which is just what her mother wants, to be relieved of her anxiety. But instead (as is quite obvious to an outsider but not to someone engaged in the child–parent relationship), she anxiously asks her to walk away ... but not to walk away.

As well as being extremely sensitive in this respect, children can also be very demanding themselves. I know personally of an unfortunate child who forced his mother to be constantly with him; otherwise he would stage monstrous crises of panic which threw all the adults into confusion. He managed to engineer it so that his mother was – literally – by his side throughout nursery school and primary school, right up to the age of eleven, when the headmaster of the private school he was attending finally decided to put a stop to it, saying that he could no longer continue to have a mother sitting at a school desk acting as bodyguard to her son. What people did not see so clearly was that the child was also being required to act as bodyguard to his mother!

This is an extreme case, it is true, but Cub and Brownie leaders could tell you a thing or two about occasions when outings first include a night spent away from home. In the evening, in their tents – or even during the day, courtesy of the unwelcome umbilical cord of the mobile phone – they are witness to desperate appeals, terrible homesickness and other unexpected forms of behaviour (bed-wetting or inexplicable eating problems, for instance) totally out of keeping with the day's other activities. Quite probably, the children concerned have parents who are in need of reassurance, even though – in theory – the parents would be the first to say that separation is a necessary "medicine" to encourage independence. They may well say: "It will do the child good," but they soon realise that it is a bitter medicine to take.

Though families pay lip-service to the principle of "each to his or her own bed", it is often disregarded for reasons which all have the same common denominator. One mother, who was very perceptive in expressing her need not to be separated from her child, posed the question: "But can we be sure that the child, left alone in his own bed, is not suffering? May he not be wondering: 'Why must I stay here on my own while they, Mummy and Daddy, are together?'" You can be quite sure that, sooner or later, the child of parents like these will indeed ask: "Why can't I come to bed with you? I'm all alone in my room (though maybe with a little brother!)."

Thanks to the blind determination with which human beings seem set on complicating their lives, we have seen a whole range of solutions adopted to avoid separation: one enormous bed, on the ground, so that the parents and three children could all sleep in the same room; double beds in parents' and children's bedrooms, justified with the words: "That way we use only king-sized sheets; it's so much simpler!"; or single beds everywhere, including the parents' bedroom (democracy insinuates itself everywhere!); or (the most common situation) one parent kicked out permanently to sleep in the child's bed, because the child has taken possession of the parental double bed – and sleeping three in a bed is so uncomfortable. These are all ingenious ways of avoiding actual separation, whilst paying lip-service to the principle of individual autonomy. It should be said that, nowadays, even fathers are becoming fierce defenders of non-separation, if not the secret promoters of "passionate togetherness".

Suffering is a precondition of maturity

What, then, is the reason for these covert operations to avoid separation? Why do people try so hard – and generally unsuccessfully – to go against one of life's basic principles? One answer must be that they do not accept – or do not want to accept – that separation involves an element of suffering. It is the element of suffering that we are reluctant to face.

Our culture – if I may digress slightly – seems always to be teaching us that we must do away with suffering in every form, that suffering must be banished as if it were a great obstacle. We have been conditioned to think that where there is suffering something must be wrong, and therefore the old idea of training ourselves to face suffering is somehow out of date. It may be because this idea accords with the myth of the "superman"; or because we have been told to break free of the shackles of masochism or the concept of sacrifice; or because, in the technological world to which we are increasingly adapting, a failure in the functioning of a mechanism means that something is wrong. The idea that growing up, maturing or simply living in this world necessarily involves suffering is something we are conditioned to resist with all our might. And yet, if we do not learn to accept times of suffering as part and parcel of growing up, we shall find ourselves – albeit involuntarily – saying no to life itself.

Let us analyse the example of Sylvia's mother. She cannot keep away from the school gate, where her daughter is "imprisoned", because she cannot tolerate even the smallest degree of suffering resulting from their separation. She might say to herself: "I'll stay at home here (and perhaps even spend my time doing something interesting!) even though I suffer a bit from not knowing how my child is getting on at the moment. I accept the slight suffering of not being with her. I am sure that accepting this small suffering will enable me to let go of my daughter a bit. I have given her her own space and that will be good for her, even if she does need me."

As regards her daughter's reluctance to tell her what has happened at school, she might also accept the slight pain involved with the thought: "It is understandable that my daughter is not willing to speak to me at present; I won't insist; I'm sure she realises I'm interested in what is going on, so she'll speak to me when she's ready."

The way some parents interrogate their children conceals the fact that they are wanting to be "fed". It is as if the parent were saying: "Tell me something to overcome my boredom with life. Give me some reason for living; I've lost my own along the way."

Instead of interrogating her daughter, Sylvia's mother could tell her what she herself has been doing: what she did during the morning; an interesting meeting she had with someone; what she has been cooking. If what her mother tells her conveys the idea: "You see, our being apart was not a bad thing; on the contrary"; or more positively: "I was really looking forward to your coming home so that I could tell you about it", without there having to be any "payback" (now you tell me something about yourself), then Sylvia will learn that separation is not a permanent loss.

Sylvia – and all children at varying stages of development who are having to come to terms with the world – can also learn that the suffering of separation is valuable in many ways. There will be times when she has to learn to defend herself; times when the person who interprets the world to her ("This is happening to you because ...", "Now you should do things in such and such a way") is not available and therefore she has to work out meanings for herself ("The teacher did not look at my drawing because I'm not the only one in the class") and so on; times when she feels she compares badly with someone else (her friend speaks more fluently than her or has a nicer school bag) and has to take second place; times when, if she wants something from a friend, she will have to come to terms with her. There will be many instances of this kind and each of these growing pains will train her to get the best out of life. She should not be allowed to avoid them in some way. The harvest will be truly plentiful when these little seeds of suffering come to fruition. When adults take it upon themselves to spare a child such sufferings, they are in fact only complicating things and acting as the greatest possible obstacle to life.

The importance of establishing a proper distance

Separation, then, with all the pain it brings, is an essential part of life, but life makes up for it by providing an abundance of new relationships. A relationship is desirable and fruitful to the extent to which it has been preceded by a separation. The separation of course requires that we leave something behind, demands discernment and decision, but it is never an end in itself and eventually results in a higher form of relationship.

The very structure of our most significant relationships requires that we make continual adjustments to them. As they become increasingly independent and find their way in life, children (and adults) must set aside the expectation of being cared for in childish ways if they are to experience more appropriate forms of care. The time will eventually come when the relationship is "reversed"; in old age, it is the parent who will be cared for by the child. And we are all aware as human beings that the highest form of care, the best relationship of all, is undoubtedly gratitude. "Owe one another nothing, except the debt of love."

Therefore, if we accept the element of legitimate suffering which separation brings – and here I repeat that there are many, many forms of separation (not least those associated with "the first time": the first time children feed themselves, go to nursery school, take the train alone, takes an exam, their first kiss and so on) – not only is the relationship not lost but it is restored on a higher plane. Establishing a proper distance does not mean plunging into a dark night of fear and loneliness, but rediscovering each other in different ways and different contexts, more aware and more mature.

Let me tell you a story ...

First night away from home

Laura looked at Frederica with new eyes. They had already had many adventures together and thoroughly enjoyed themselves. To tell the truth, she had always seen Frederica as prettier, more attractive and having more things than her, which made her a bit envious. When she climbed into Frederica's mother's car to spend an afternoon with her friend, she felt rather small, because the car was so luxurious compared with her mother's Fiat Panda. Frederica also had a rather dreamy, ladylike appearance – for instance when she sat at the piano, which she had begun to study a year or more ago. The teachers had even said that Frederica could play a piano solo at their class-leaving performance (they were in the last year of primary school).

The two girls had gone on the year's first Cub outing together. In this department, Laura was already a veteran. She was already in her second year as a Cub (the leaders had decided to call all the children Cubs, as there were only four girls but thirteen boys in the pack). It was Laura who had suggested that her friend should become a Cub. Frederica's mother had needed a great deal of reassurance. She had spoken to the leaders, one by one. She had got them to explain what activities were involved. In short, she "left nothing to chance", as she put it. Frederica seemed enthusiastic about everything to do with scouting; Laura had certainly aroused her interest.

So here they were on their first "short" outing, as the leaders called it: Saturday afternoon, a night under canvas and everyone back home before lunch on Sunday. For the evening, everyone had been asked to bring a packed meal and, the moment they arrived, all the provisions were stored away together, to be brought out and eaten at dusk. For some reason, Frederica had been thinking of the evening meal all afternoon while they were playing games. Her mother had prepared her a magnificent picnic basket full of goodies, including chocolates, which she was not usually so generous with. "You never know," she thought as she was preparing the hamper.

But, wonder of wonders, all the provisions were set out together in the middle of a big tablecloth by the "cooks", and they sat round cross-legged on the ground in a big circle, really like famished wolf-cubs. Each got up in turn (the leaders were quite inflexible in applying the rules) and chose three things from the pile in the middle. When Frederica's turn came, the delicious rolls prepared by her mother had already gone. She found some other very tasty items, which seemed strange to her taste. She ate and ate, because she was really hungry; if her mother had seen her, she would have been astonished. Laura kept an eye on her and generously managed to save her a chocolate, which Frederica found even better than usual.

As night fell, the tents waited to engulf the weary campers. The tent in which the four girls were to sleep was right in the middle of the camp. The fire round which they had sat to sing their songs had burned down to glowing embers. Their sleeping bags were a bit damp, but nice and soft. Frederica could not remember ever having been so tired. But she was unable to get to sleep.

"Aren't you asleep?" asked Laura, who had the eyes of a cat and the sensitivity of a ferret.

"No, I feel like crying," Frederica suddenly blurted out.

Laura sat up with a start: "You feel like crying? Is something hurting you?"

"Hurting? No. But I feel sort of heavy …"

"I told you you were eating too much," said Laura, who was already preparing to call Akela.

"No, my stomach is fine …"

"Why are you feeling heavy, then?" asked Laura curiously.

"Tell me, when did you go on your first outing?"

"When I was almost ten," said Laura proudly. "Are you wondering if I felt like crying?"

"Yes."

"No, I was too tired and too happy."

"But what about your mother … Did you think she was sleeping?"

"Of course," smiled Laura, "why would she have stayed awake?"

"You think my mother will be asleep?"

"Of course. Why not? It's almost midnight."

"If only I had a mobile phone."

"Mobile phones aren't allowed on camp, you know."

"If I had a mobile phone, I'd give her a ring …"

"In that case, you'd wake her up!" replied Laura, down to earth as usual.

Her remark seemed to strike a chord with her friend.

"You're right, I'd wake her up ... and, if she wakes up, she can't get back to sleep again."

"I tell you what," suggested Laura, wanting to be helpful, "when you get home tomorrow, ask her if she slept all right."

"OK, then. Now I'll try to sleep."

"That's right, Frederica," said Laura.

But a few minutes later, Laura whispered to her friend: "Pst ... pst ... Are you asleep?"

"What is it?"

"I just wanted to say, I didn't cry the first time, but I was a bit afraid!"

Things to talk about with your child
- What happens to Frederica on her first night away from home, without her parents?
- Why can't Frederica get to sleep?
- What do the two friends learn from the experience?

Chapter Six

The sufferings of the adoptive child

Case study

Francisco was perfectly at ease in class III E, a bundle of fun and energy. Without his being aware of it, his black, tightly curled hair and dark complexion, broad grinning mouth, unusual almond-shaped eyes and carefree, cheerful gestures made him both distinctive and reassuring. One day, the girl who sat beside him, who was rather shy and reserved, accommodating and friendly in her quiet way, suddenly asked him: "Why are you called 'Francisco' and not 'Francis'?"

"And why are you called 'Martina'?" he replied, not knowing the answer to her question.

"I don't know," answered Martina in all honesty.

Children are generally quite content in the certainty of not knowing.

The new history teacher, however, wanted to get off to a good start and, determined to teach history in a concrete way, had drawn up an ambitious plan: each child was to gather all possible data concerning his or her personal history, look out all the available documents, then produce an attractive poster to show to the rest of the class. Then she intended to ask the children – as historians – to look at, interpret and narrate the history documented in the three best and most accurate posters.

The class reacted with great enthusiasm, Francisco included. Each went home with a battery of questions, primed to carry out his or her investigation: when and where was I born; who was present at my birth; how much did I weigh and how long was I; did I have any distinctive marks; was I the first (second, third and so on) child in my family; who chose my name and why; when was I baptised; what was the first word I uttered; when did I take my first steps; and so on and so forth. Of course, the answers were to be supported by all the photographs, video clips and "artefacts" the children could lay their hands on, as in any proper investigation. The second stage was to draw a family tree, beginning with parents and working back to grandparents, great-grandparents and, if possible, great-great-grandparents and even remoter ancestors.

At home that afternoon, Francisco talked enthusiastically about his new homework, but he could see that his mother was not very comfortable about it.

"Where are the photos of me when I was a baby?"

"Um ... you know that we adopted you when you were three years old."

"Yes, I know, but we do have some photographs, don't we?" It was difficult for an eight-year-old to hold together in his mind two conflicting ideas: the teacher's request, which he saw as quite normal; and his own very individual past, which was different from that of his school-mates.

"Listen, Francisco," said his mother finally, "this is a serious matter; we'll talk about it when your father gets home."

His adoptive parents in fact discussed the matter at length. They were somewhat surprised by the teacher's request, because they had made no secret of Francisco's adopted status, and they felt that they could not leave Francisco "defenceless" in front of the rest of the class.

"We'll have to find an honourable solution," said his father.

"The best thing would be to go and talk it over with the teacher."

"What could we say? She would object that she is well aware of the situation but cannot have her whole teaching programme disrupted by the fact that there is one child in the class who does not have a record of his past."

"I still think that's what we should ask her to do."

"But now she has already launched the project …"

"I know; that's what is so difficult about it."

"Then we must find an honourable solution for our Francisco. I don't want him to feel different from the others. I want him to feel equal to everyone else."

"So what can we do: give him the photo of the neighbour's new-born baby?" his mother suggested with a smile.

"It's no joking matter. He has a family for all practical purposes, hasn't he? So he can talk about us, our grandparents, when we came to live here and so on, just like all the others."

"And what shall we do about the baby photos? And the question about the first words he uttered?"

"There's no need to complicate everything … I know … We've got some magnificent photographs of us coming off the aeroplane. Here we are. You look beautiful in this one, coming down the steps holding his hand … And here's another one, of when we celebrated his first birthday with us."

And so, with Francisco's help, his father created a magnificent, carefully documented poster, into which he put all his enthusiasm and artistic talent. It was quite clear how "the world had begun" for Francisco – and for his mother and father.

When the great day came, because it was a special occasion he took his son to school in the car, so that the poster would not get crumpled. He helped Francisco take it into the classroom and, when the teacher and pupils began to gather round, made his exit, feeling pleased with himself.

Displayed on the wall with all the others, Francisco's brightly coloured poster attracted everyone's attention. It was undoubtedly the best and the teacher took the opportunity to praise him to the skies. But Francisco's sharp ears soon heard giggles and comments from other parts of the classroom: "Look, look, Francisco was born in an aeroplane!"

The next day, he heard his dear friend Martina whisper to another little girl: "My mummy told me that poor Francisco is nobody's child."

"Then his mummy and daddy are not his real parents," concluded the other girl.

Francisco, who at first had looked with pride on the poster his father had made, began to feel ill at ease. The aeroplane he was pictured emerging from suddenly looked more like a sinister bird, a vulture, something hostile. He knew, of course, that he was adopted, but the word had not meant much to him. His mother had explained that he had been carried in the tummy of another mother, but he so loved the mother he knew that he had not given it much thought. Now he was discovering that she was not his "real" mother – and his father was not his "real" father, either.

For the first time, his normally carefree mind was full of questions which weighed like lead. Who were his "real" mother and father? Why had he no memories of them? Why had they abandoned him? Wouldn't he ever see them again? He even had the impression that his friend Martina was looking at him in a strange way, as she never had before. And so were the others. And suddenly he felt anger well up in him, making him want to shout (though he was careful not to do so; he no longer trusted them): "Why are you looking at me like that? I'll tear your eyes out!"

When the teacher asked him: "Can you explain your magnificent poster to the others in the class?" he answered: "No, definitely not," and withdrew into a sulk, thinking: "Damn it! I don't trust them." At this, the teacher made a great effort to explain to his companions, who were all ears, that Francisco was in fact an adoptive child; and that he had been fortunate to find such a nice family, with parents who loved him so much.

But there came a point when she noticed that he had covered his ears.

The grown-ups discussed the matter among themselves, each trying to convince themselves that they were right. As far as the teacher was concerned, it was clear that the poster project, which brought Francisco's adoptive status out into the open, was helpful in making him more aware of the fact and conveyed an important message to the rest of the class: they must learn not to discriminate. In any case, Francisco was liked by everyone. For his father, the idea of the aeroplane had been brilliant, enabling his son to present his own poster, just like everyone else. The only one who harboured any doubts was his mother, because she was aware of a sudden change in the boy.

Over the next few weeks, the change became evident to everyone. His natural exuberance had been replaced by a compulsion to be naughty and seek attention by agitation and disobedience. His homework deteriorated. And so began the tellings off: "But why are you behaving like this?", "Come on now, calm down!", "Stay at your desk!", "Pay attention! Stop distracting the others!", "Listen, do you want a black mark?", "You're a pain ... You're always making trouble!"

At home, too, he was always being corrected, especially by his father, who said: "Black marks? Since when have you been getting black marks for misbehaviour? I'll have to come and talk to the teachers."

If he had been able to talk about the anger he was feeling, Francisco would have said: "You asked for it. Well, now you're all going to have to pay!"

The wound that cannot be denied

Are we really prepared for an adoption? It is pointless if we, as adults, only put our efforts into preparing the child, trying to integrate him or her, making the child feel at home in our culture and in our family (depending on whether the child is from overseas or from closer to home). Inherent in adoption is a hurt which it is pointless and harmful to deny – a hurt which no triumphalism, no appeal to realism, no declaration of egalitarianism can possibly allay, even when we are totally committed to making an adoption work.

And the hurt does not lie – as it might seem to at first sight – with the sterility of the couple who are adopting the child. Of course, this too is a grief which has to be worked through; and on its satisfactory resolution will depend to a large extent the success of the adoption. But the real hurt is something else: the fact that it was not possible for a little human being to be brought up by his or her own parents; that the child should have been deprived of the warmth of a natural family and the basic necessities of life; that to utter the words "mummy" and "daddy" he or she had to cross land and sea. All of us are to some extent responsible for this hurt: for the fact that there are unjust societies, founded on discrimination and violence and the appropriation of resources by the few to the detriment of the poverty-stricken many; that there are desperate people left to fend for themselves, rejected and exploited. All these things should concern us and make us question our consciences (including, of course, those who have not the slightest intention of becoming adoptive parents).

Adoption is the consequence of a hurt, a wound for which the child is the first to have to pay. No couple, however good their preparation or strong their marriage, can do away with the reality of this wound. Ask yourself: "Even if a child deprived of parents could be taken in by close relatives he or she knows and loves, would this compensate for the loss and make the child happy?"

So to claim to be able to wipe away this hurt with the words: "You are fortunate to have ended up with us", is adding insult to injury. And the additional triumphant tone of: "Look how worthy we are, as parents, for coming and taking you in; and how good we are, as a school, because we talk about it openly and do not discriminate against you", in fact disguises the violence implicit in the idea: "Really, you should be thanking us."

The trap of omnipotence

But if we adults prepared ourselves for an adoption (not just the adoptive parents, but all of us), we would find ourselves feeling grateful to the child. We would regard the child with great humility, as if to say: "Thank you for coming among us. Because you have allowed yourself to be adopted, we adults experience a degree of forgiveness: you have allowed yourself to be embraced by strangers; you have accepted that an aeroplane catapulted you into another world; you have opened your ears to a new language; you have begun to forget the old wounds; you have smiled, given us kisses and begun to trust again; and so you have come to know us, with what are for you the new names of mummy, daddy, teacher, friend and cousin. We, the adult world, accept the fact that this new kinship and these new relationships are rooted in suffering. We apologise to you that it is so. We are grateful to you – but not in order to make concessions to you or call you 'poor child', treat you in a patronising way or transform you into a tyrant." Recognising a hurt does not mean wallowing in guilt; rather, it means restraining oneself from telling or believing fairy tales or nostrums which put a sugar coating on reality but do not change it – and so turn out to be traps.

If she had approached things from this angle, the teacher's project could have been beneficial for all concerned. The most violent aspect of our (unfortunately, true) story was not the fact that no notice was given and that the school did not involve the family, nor the parents consult the school. This was, of course, deplorable; each party left the other to manage on its own; each behaved as if operating on tramlines, as if the child were not the end on which the educational efforts of the various adults concerned should be focused. The school seemed to be saying: We must implement our teaching programme, which is for everyone; what does it matter if a child (only one!) has special needs? Someone will pick up the pieces. The family seemed to be saying: How can we ward off the blow and protect our child? How can we do what the school wants without it harming him? How can we show that we are superman and superwoman? As a result, neither party questioned the nice fiction of school–family co-operation and addressed the other about the reality of the situation. And so Francisco was left to "expose" his unique condition: how he was born (originated, had his beginning) from an aeroplane.

The trap of oversimplification

However, as I was saying, this was not the most violent aspect of the story. The worst thing was that neither family nor school took into account the difficult change in relationships between Francisco and his companions that was bound to result from the poster exercise. School and family all too often indulge in a strange "abstraction" strategy: they abstract children from their social situation, overlooking the fact that their relationship with their peers is the context in which their real learning takes place.

In this case, the learning which the teacher – legitimately – seeks to bring about is to do with the succession of real events of which history is constituted; history is never abstract. But the fact that Francisco was "born from an aeroplane" – to quote the highly effective expression used by one of his companions – makes it impossible to test the continuity of history. This piece of information should not be passed over in silence but set in its true context in the writing of Francisco's personal history. We would rightly condemn a historian who forced life to conform to his or her preconceived framework and took no account of anything outside it!

Since the adult world neglects its responsibilities, not ascribing due value to diversity, Francisco's peers are left to interpret his story with the instruments available to them (which unfortunately reflect the subtle, implicit forms of discrimination of the adult world). In other words, being born from an aeroplane is not something interesting which raises further questions and demands further explanation. No, he is different – full stop – and is labelled as such. It is not a case of "this friend of ours comes from a distant country and that is something interesting", but "this child is not one of us" – full stop.

Then there is a tendency to put a patronising gloss on the fact that Francisco "is not one of us". On the one hand, he is "nobody's child" (or not the child of someone like us); on the other, "his parents are not his 'real' parents". Note that no one voices the questions that are bound to spring to mind; children are very sensitive to the fact that certain questions are out of bounds.

Suddenly, Francisco is alienated from his school-mates. He feels he is a stranger: before he was "one of us"; now his place is elsewhere. It is not that previously his companions (and he himself) were unaware that he was different physically, but the difference was not in contradiction with his being "one of us" – just as, for example, the reddish coloration of one chick in a brood of yellow chicks does not prevent its being fully part of the group. So, in this way, Francisco and his companions are robbed of the wholeness of their relationship.

It is worth emphasising that his companions have also been robbed. They have been robbed of the opportunity to broaden the field of "being one of us" – a field that can become wide enough to include someone "born in a distant country".

What, then, should the teacher have done (apart from consulting her colleagues) before launching her history project? Having obtained the consent of the family, she could have said something roughly like this: "We are going to do some research into our origins ... And because we are in a special situation, I want to explain one or two things to you so that we can all feel at ease. I want to tell you a story that is rather different from yours: the story of our Francisco (or, Francisco's father and mother will come and tell you about it, if he prefers). His father and mother went to find him in a distant country and they are very grateful to him because, although he was born there, he has come and adapted to living among us. We shall also be looking at the beauty and the problems of the place where Francisco was born because he can bring photographs of his country and tell us about it, while of course he cannot bring the baby photos and other things you will be able to bring ... So in our class this investigation of our origins will certainly not be boring or ordinary." This kind of approach would not have robbed Francisco's companions of the right to know and accept what is different, but would have triggered a genuine mutual thankfulness.

The trap of words

But the one who has been robbed of most in all this is Francisco himself. He had struggled manfully to weave a web of relationships with his peers, with all the ups and downs that this process implies.

Then, suddenly, he experiences the unspoken suffering of no longer being one with his peers. Francisco is no longer perceived in the same way; the world has suddenly changed. The aeroplane becomes a sinister bird, his adoption an act of robbery. With good reason, he would like to "tear out the eyes" of those around him, to prevent them from looking at him in a way that makes him feel different.

With good reason, he covers his ears when faced with the teacher's demands and her clumsy attempts to explain it all.

He has drawn his own conclusions; he no longer trusts them. It is the saddest possible event in the life of the child; the pain is unbearable. Now he has to watch his back; he can no longer have confidence that what an adult says is for his good. How does Francisco react to this pain? Quite unconsciously, he shields himself from it by becoming angry: "You grown-ups cannot reach the pain I am feeling (you don't deserve to) because I am using my anger to cover it up. How could I tell you that I suddenly feel so much fear and anguish; that I am left with nothing steady, safe and stable, now that my companions (those who think like me and view the world as I do) are secretly saying among themselves that my father and mother are not 'real'? I am filled with an anxiety and agitation that compel me to behave 'badly'; nothing is right any more; there is no longer anything I can rest in."

From the adults' reaction to the (for them, inexplicable) change in Francisco's behaviour, it is clear that he again is the one who must pay the price. The best the grown-ups can do is to scold him, thereby confirming him in the now invasive suspicion that: "I am badly made; I am a 'bastard' [the very affective term spontaneously used by one girl to define herself when she discovered that she was adopted]; I cannot be like the others."

Let us clear our mind of the romantic illusion that all that needs to be done is for someone to sit Francisco on their knee and ask him lovingly: "Why are you behaving like this? What has gone wrong?" He would make no reply. Firstly, because he lacks the means of expression, it is most unlikely that he will have made a link between the poster (and his companions' interpretation of it) and the anger and agitation he feels. Secondly, even if he has made a vague connection, he would not say so, because he is experiencing the profound unease of no longer trusting people.

The adults (or at least one of them) will have to go through a much sterner test if they are to reach him now. They will need to tell him by their behaviour, and not just in fine words: "It is good that you are here, just as you are, including your angry feelings; what we wanted was not a good boy but you yourself, and we would not change you for anything in the world." Of course, this does not mean letting him do anything he wants (wrong behaviour still has to be corrected with firmness), but the message conveyed to the child is: "You are not your behaviour; you are you, and we like you as you are." This is the only way Francisco will come to understand that adults are more than the sum of their mistakes!

Who is the saviour?

I must make the point again: we cannot get round the hurt that underlies every adoption – and which opens us up to gratitude and joy at having the child. This should prevent us from imposing further hurts and needless sufferings. Even in the case of fostering, there is no hiding the painful fact that in our societies there are families which have failed and therefore there are children who need to be "lent" parents who will give them a second chance. The same sort of attitude is required of us when we come into contact with a child from a deprived background. Deprived children, who experience the bitterness of not having the same rights as others, come in different shapes and sizes: the children of immigrants; the children of those who are unemployed and homeless; children who have lost one parent; children whose parents are in prison; children with no father. Let us respect the courage of all those who work with deprived children and take responsibility for them. We are grateful to them and pray that they will never use fairy stories as a way of minimising the pain involved.

Let me tell you a story ...

Sharing a mother half and half?

Mark had never enjoyed so much attention. The RE teacher had asked him (having obtained the permission of everybody concerned) to tell the third and fifth years his news, as well as his own class – the second years – who were obviously the best informed.

"What's he like?" asked his close friends.

"He's good looking, but a bit thin," replied Mark with an expert air.

"Can he speak?"

"Of course, he can speak; he's not an animal."

"But what language does he speak?"

"He has learned a few words of Portuguese; and so have I."

"How come? Did you go to Brazil as well?"

"No, but my mother taught me."

"What's his name?"

"He's called Paul."

"Will you take us to see him?"

"He's not an exhibit," said Mark seriously, "he's my little brother."

This reply silenced Mark's friends for the time being.

"But does he know he's your brother?" Lydia asked him during break.

She wanted to explore the subject from all angles; it is not every day you have a friend who has acquired a new little brother.

"I don't know," answered Mark, who was nothing if not honest.

"But have you told him? Where does he sleep? What does he call you? What does he eat?" asked the girls, who had gathered round.

Mark had never felt so important, but he was rather frightened by all these questions.

"He sleeps with me," he said, choosing to answer the easiest question. "Last night, Mummy put his bed beside mine," he added proudly.

"Why?"

"Because he was crying and couldn't get to sleep."

"And what did you do?" Lydia asked, agog with curiosity.

"I held his hand."

"And did he go to sleep?"

"Yes."

Lydia looked at him as if he were a snake charmer.

"But is he very little?"

"He's little, yes; he's only three."

"My little brother is three, as well," said Louise at this point, "but he's naughty."

"Is Paul naughty, too?" asked Lydia again.

"No, Paul isn't. But Mummy told me he feels very out of his element, because he's only been with us a week. Perhaps he doesn't yet feel confident enough to be naughty."

"What does 'out of his element' mean?"

"It means this isn't his country, doesn't it?" said Christine, who had been silent up to that point.

"I don't know," answered Mark, who was very perceptive, "perhaps it means he feels a bit foreign."

"Exactly," interjected Christine, "he comes from another country."

"But is your mother his mother, too?" asked Lydia suddenly, struck by this new idea.

Fortunately, the bell for the end of break rang at that moment and Mark had no time to reply.

Later that day, at home, Mark wore a worried expression as he ate his meal, though his appetite was as good as ever.

"What's the matter?" asked his mother tenderly, aware that he had something on his mind.

"Who is Paul's mother?" burst out Mark.

"Who is Paul's brother?" asked his mother in reply.

"I am."

"And who is Paul's father?"

"Daddy is," replied Mark, thinking of his own father.

"And who is Paul's grandmother?"

"Grandma is."

"So, who is Paul's mother?"

"You are."

"You see, we're a family; since Paul came, our family has grown. Thanks to him."

"But didn't he have a mother of his own?"

Mark's mother resisted the temptation to say: "I've explained this to you a dozen times," and understood what was behind her son's question. She took him on her lap and said: "I'll always be your mother."

"Yes."

"There was a woman who was Paul's mother for the first nine months of his life. She carried him in her tummy until he was born, but she wasn't able to be his mother for life."

"Why?"

"We don't know; if she had been able to, I'm sure she would have done," she said calmly, making room on her lap for little Paul, who had just joined them. "But he has been so kind as to come and join our family, and so you can be his brother, I can be his mother and Daddy can be his father," she added, hugging them both.

Next morning, without even saying hello, Mark immediately announced to Lydia: "My mummy will always be my mummy. But she is also Paul's mummy."

"What?" asked Lydia in surprise, having forgotten her question of the day before.

"What are you two chattering about?" asked the teacher.

"I asked Mark who was the mother of his little brother," admitted Lydia, who had suddenly remembered her question.

"Oh!" said the teacher, somewhat embarrassed. "And what did Mark say?"

For the teacher's benefit, Mark repeated out loud what he had said: "I said: 'My mummy will always be my mummy. But now she is also Paul's mummy, because he has come to live with us.'"

"That's a very good answer, Mark. You know, you have helped me to understand something."

Mark, Lydia, Christine and all the others observed the teacher quizzically.

"You have helped me understand that Mark has not lost his mother, nor does he have to share her half and half." She laughed: "It's just that now she is Paul's mother, too."

And, quite spontaneously, all of them broke into applause.

> ***Things to talk about with your child***
> – Why does Mark feel important?
> – What does he think of his little brother?
> – Is it true that he does not have to share his mother half and half?

PART THREE

SUFFERING THAT CAN BE AVOIDED

The stories of Hugh, David and Irma clearly illustrate that a great deal of suffering is avoidable. Without entering into the field of pathological child abuse, we find many situations in which a child's suffering is literally inflicted by those who are responsible for bringing him or her up. In discussing such situations, it is not my intention to blame the parents or close relatives concerned (let us leave that to the tabloids!), but to show – in confident hope of better things – that the gratuitous suffering inflicted on a child is almost always unintentional. It therefore comes as a great relief when one learns to recognise it and free oneself of its power. In any case, "error" (in this field) is not the same as "guilt"; and the healthiest situation is not when parents do not make mistakes in the first place (if this is ever really the case), but when they learn from their mistakes.

The kind of suffering we are concerned with here occurs when we saddle children with our own disappointments, require them to compensate for our hurts, deny them the right to exist or desperately want them to be different. It occurs when we require children to take our side against our partner or other close relatives; or leave them totally at the mercy of their own mood swings and misfortunes. The resulting burden of suffering is avoidable; and we may well find that the comfort we receive from children when we do what is right far exceeds our expectations.

In particular, we shall be trying to answer some disturbing questions: how do you avoid making children bear the burden of your own difficulties? How can you be open with them about your problems and at the same time not draw them in? How do you cope with your feelings of guilt when you cannot give your children all the things you would like to? How do you avoid requiring them to behave and think in a way that is beyond their years?

Chapter Seven

When a child feels unwanted

Case study

Hugh felt as if his heart were being crushed; until then, he had never imagined one could feel such pain. And yet, he was ten years old and his little heart had already had to bear its share of griefs, especially his father's long illness. Even when his father had been at home, he had seemed isolated by his illness; despite Hugh's restless nature, he had taken little interest in the boy, who had been born some years after his two sisters and was a small, sickly child. And yet, there had been moments when his father was more cheerful (and then it was as if the sun were shining in the house) and would sit Hugh beside him on the settee and tell him long stories – so long that Hugh would lose the thread. Maybe his father was talking for his own benefit, but how pleasant and reassuring it was to hear him speaking, hear his voice and be convinced – mistakenly maybe – that the voice was speaking just for him.

He had prayed and prayed that his father would be present for his first communion. He would have liked to have both parents there in church, sitting behind him, just like his friends. But it was not to be. Instead, his uncle and his mother had taken him to the hospital to show the certificate to his father. Hugh had been the centre of attention for a few moments, then the grown-ups had begun to discuss their own affairs: illness, medicines, the cost of treatment, needs, problems and sorrows.

His father died when he was nine; and even that grief had been bearable. He remembered his father's coffin being brought out of the hospital mortuary; saw the adults wiping away their tears and comforting one another with the words: "At last, his sufferings are over." He saw the wreaths of flowers and the earth being shovelled into the grave. The priest had stroked his hair and invited him more warmly than he normally did to attend Sunday school. And someone had said: "Now, you're the little man of the house."

But he was a very, very lonely little man. His mother was fully taken up with running the mobile cheese stall. She had never imagined she would have to live this way, surrounded by the smell of cheese – which she hated – visiting the remote villages of their valley, where only the old folk now wanted to buy her wares. The customers were loyal, but very slow in paying, and though she was slowly paying off the business debts – unlike her husband, who had allowed the customers credit and practically given the cheese away – it was gradually draining her energies.

Her elder daughter had no intention of helping out. There would have been some comfort if she had been making progress at school but instead she preferred to hang around with her friends. Her second daughter was a great support – rather like herself in character. At the age of sixteen, she had decided to leave school and help her mother; she got up early every morning, did all the lifting and carrying and had an unfailing memory for the customers and what they owed. Her mother could not have managed without her, though she was well aware of what her daughter was sacrificing in the process.

But none of these things was a source of unbearable grief for Hugh. Not until he heard his mother say: "You were a mistake" did he experience a pain he could not cope with.

It had been just like any other day in his final year at primary school – a grey, boring day, as he tried to cope with a steady stream of orders and corrections: "Hugh, you must stay awake", "Hugh, it's your turn", "Hugh, you need to apply yourself more", "Hugh, you will never get anywhere in maths if you don't pay attention", "Hugh, you've got it all wrong again." The school bus had brought him home bearing a demerit form – one of the many his mother had signed for him – stating: "Hugh is inattentive and makes no effort." On this occasion, he had presented it himself, handing his mother his school diary, without waiting for his second sister to discover it (she normally tried to relieve her mother of the task of supervising Hugh, as well as doing all the other jobs she had to do). His mother had looked at the diary as if it were something disgusting and said, with finality: "You were a mistake." She then added the usual string of complaints, which Hugh knew by heart: "I despair of you. You'll never achieve anything. You're just like your father. As if I haven't enough troubles already! Why don't you make an effort? Why don't you get a grip on yourself? Why do you bring me nothing but worries? You could easily try a bit harder."

But, that day, she had pronounced her final verdict: "You were a mistake."

Hugh did not think to watch his mother's face as she was saying it; he did not know if she was desperately sad or simply angry and resentful. But from that day on, Hugh saw himself in a new way. That sentence was like a shovelful of mud that was permanently stuck to him. Children like Hugh have generally learned to defend themselves, at least by thinking such thoughts as:

"It's you that's nasty."

"What am I supposed to do about it, since you had me?"

"You've no cause to hurt me like that."

"It's you that are deficient as a mother."

"It's you that don't love me."

"Who asked you to give birth to me?"

But even if one of these sentences did rise to his lips, we can be sure that, in his heart of hearts, he was not confident of his "defensive armour".

Although he appeared not to take hold of his mother's words, he was profoundly convinced that he had not been wanted. What she had said penetrated his being like a corrosive poison. If he had been able to express himself, Hugh would have said: "OK, I understand. I was a mistake; you didn't want me; I've no right to exist; my birth was a misfortune; there's nothing I can do about it; I'm to blame, full stop. Everything I do will be wrong; I'll never do anything right; I'll always be useless; no one will like me."

At this point, Hugh had two roads open to him: either he could withdraw into his shell and try not to exist, acting in a conformist way but without much success (and his regressive behaviour will confirm the adult's opinion that he is a liability); or he could protest against the debt he could never pay: "Since I'll never be able to satisfy you, I might as well go off the rails as it suits me."

Hugh chose the second alternative (and of course confirmed his mother's opinion of him).

His teachers asked his mother to come and see them.

"We've tried everything we know with your son."

"I know, he's the cross I have to bear."

"But can't you get him to do anything?"

"That's just the way he is, stubborn and disobedient. He's always out nowadays. I don't even know where he is. I can't get him to stay at home."

"We have no alternative but to fail him."

"Yes, of course. Fail him; that'll teach him. It's only to be expected, after all I've suffered already."

Hugh accepted his failure with resignation; it did not even seem to upset him. His second sister gave him a good hiding: "Aren't you ashamed to make Mum suffer like this? Can't you see everything she does for us?"

It was then that Hugh answered: "Anyway, she never wanted me."

No one realised that his words were not a challenge or a provocation, but the way in which Hugh allowed himself to express the hurt he had long been nursing, which had now eaten deep into his heart. If someone had been able to see the black hole at the back of his uncrying eyes, they would have understood.

Stop!

Let it be said straight away that no parent, whatever his or her circumstances or whatever the misdoings of the child, is entitled to make a child suffer in this way. But, of course, the fact of saying so will do nothing to help Hugh or other children in his situation.

We therefore need to try to understand the sufferings of this mother and this child – not to justify them or minimise them, but to do our bit to try and ensure that dramas of this kind occur as infrequently as possible.

Even reading stories of this kind is painful. We would prefer not to know; to think that such mothers cannot possibly exist. And so we tend to ignore injustices as things that do not concern us. But, in actual fact, we educators, parents and teachers are not always as innocent as we might like to think.

Let us try to understand the mother's loneliness and pain ...

So let us take a hard look at this mother. How is it possible that a mother can say to a child born alive and intact, however frustrating his behaviour: "You were a mistake. I didn't want to have you; I didn't want to look after you; I didn't want to make any more sacrifices, carry any more burdens"?

This mother has been left alone, terribly alone. Her husband's illness, the burden of carrying on the business, being a widow, the difficulties with her daughters (including the helpful one, because the mother feels she is asking her to make too many sacrifices) – these things are a mountain that no woman should be asked to cope with alone. It is not just the extended family network that is at fault; even if it were functioning, it might well be insufficient. We have to take issue with the social support network in the broadest sense of the term. Was there no spontaneous help from neighbours? Could not the social services have organised supervision for the child, both academically and in providing positive role models? This network seems to have been cruelly deficient.

His mother experiences her third pregnancy as a cause of "grief", resulting in yet another demand being made of her when she is already at the end of her tether. She perceives her pregnancy as a kind of injustice; even before the child was born, the mother had rejected him as unwanted. That makes her feel – more or less confusedly – guilty; no mother rejects a child casually, with impunity, because she is "equipped" to foster life, not to destroy it. Her rejection of her son is, in a way, an act of violence against herself.

Maybe for this reason, as her son grows, she collects "evidence" to justify herself. She finds the baby tiring and disruptive; the child does not develop normally – as if he were determined to make himself as much of a burden as possible. We know – in theory, at least – that a vicious circle has been created. The more the child feels he is a burden, the harder it is for him to blossom (even his vital defences are threatened and he finds nothing easy, not even feeding and/or sleeping). The more the child fails to respond to his mother's caring input, the more the mother feels in her heart that she is right ("I knew he would always be nothing more than a burden!"). She begins to reckon time in a strange and bitter way: "Since you were born ..."

"Since you were born, I have been losing my teeth"; "Since you were born, I've begun to need glasses"; "Since you were born, I've never really felt well" and so on. Once upon a time (and partly because of the lack of medical knowledge), it was more common for mothers to express themselves in this way. Sometimes there may have been an element of truth in such statements; but why make them in the first place? The implicit message seems to be: "Look, it's not my fault if I blame you for coming along; that's just the way it is!"

Nowadays, mothers have more sophisticated ways of playing the same tune: "Since you were born, I've had to give up my career; I've had no time for myself; I've neglected my marriage" and so on.

Very often, the mother concerned is not aware that "remarks" of this kind sound like accusations ("It's you who are to blame for being born!") to her child. Her intention is rather to set out her merits, or better, what she deserves in return: "Look what I've done for you", thinking that the child is bound to react by being good and well behaved and grateful. Experience teaches us that this is not likely to be the child's response, even if there are good intentions on both sides.

... as the soil in which her negative prophecy matures

And yet, in the bottom of our hearts, one insistent question still remains: why say it to him, to your son, who – it is crushingly obvious! – can do absolutely nothing about it anyway? It is not just to influence him, to force him to give up certain disappointing behaviour patterns. There is also a much deeper reason, which we need to approach with respect and a certain trepidation. By proclaiming (in an infinity of ways) that "You were a mistake", the mother is uttering a kind of prophecy against herself: "I already know I won't be a good mother to you; I know I won't be able to give you what you need; I won't manage to bring you up with any joy; and you, you will punish me; you will be exactly the opposite of all I desire." When a mother feels "punished" by her child, her rejection of the child is total; what might have been the best part of her becomes her implacable judge.

Obviously, a father can also be mired in such negative prophecies; and parents themselves may have been the object of similar prophecies on the part of their parents; maybe they were also told: "You were a mistake", even if not in so many words.

It bears repeating: parents must not be left to cope alone, especially when they have not worked through their own sufferings as children.

Negative reactions

But let us return to Hugh and the crushing pain he feels. The most painful and extreme alienation from an adult occurs when children learn to disguise their suffering, building up a mistrust which makes a deep (indelible?) mark on their heart. The adult is excluded from their internal world and becomes an enemy. The children can no longer give the adult even a crumb of themselves; they can no longer say: "I'm feeling ill", "Help me", "Why are you being unkind to me?"; they have lost all trust. As they grow up, children like this will behave without restraint, committing robbery, taking the law into their own hands, stealing or displaying moral insensitivity. They behave without restraint because they find no barrier in themselves. One woman told us how, when she was out on her own one night in a run-down part of town, she was attacked by three youths with obviously violent intentions. She was sufficiently on the ball to shout out: "Think of your mother! What would she say if she could see you?" and, turning to the one who was holding her by the arm, begged: "Think of the way your mother held you in her arms. Think how she would suffer if she could see you now! Let me go for the sake of your mother!" The young man loosed his grip, while the other two made fun of him, but the moment's hesitation was enough for her to escape.

A boy like Hugh, who has to silence his anger and fear at not being loved, gets caught up in a spiral of negative loyalty: the less he manages to satisfy his mother, the less he sees her eyes shine in his direction and the greater his despair at not coming up to her expectations. It is as if (unwittingly) he were falling in love with the negative image his mother has of him (we presume that his father also had a negative opinion of him, though in this story he is a shadowy figure in the background because of his illness; but it is unlikely that just one parent could convey so negative an impression). It is as if there is no way for him, apart from the one his mother fears he will take.

The absence of positive bonding with siblings

Nor is that all. Parents who make negative prophecies about a child (and about themselves, as we have seen in this story) will also tend to focus their children's attention on themselves and rob them of a positive bond with their siblings.

Think for a moment of the siblings in our case study. The elder daughter seems to be a total outsider, as if she had shaken off the family burdens, and in this respect she comes to serve as a model for Hugh. The second has taken on the very demanding role of substitute parent; when she takes notice of Hugh it is from the position of deputy mother. Therefore Hugh is deprived of his two sisters; he has no fraternal bond with them and he himself deprives them of himself as a brother. He seems entirely focused, initially, on trying to attract the attention of his ailing father, then on attracting the disapproval of his mother. In families of this kind, it is as if each child were obliged to relate singly with their father and mother. Horizontal relationships are not allowed, implicitly forbidden; forming alliances is taboo; the children do not even know how to go about it, because each concentrates on engaging the parents and wrestling with them.

Difficulties in forming gratifying relationships with siblings are a further significant source of suffering. "At least," one young man said to me, "when Mum and Dad used to quarrel, my sister and I would sit and hug each other on the settee." Brotherly or sisterly love can be a balm for wounded souls. In addition, relations with peers are greatly helped by the fact of having learned to form healthy bonds on equal terms with siblings – another potential advantage of which little Hugh was robbed.

One final point, which I hardly need to make: it is obvious that Hugh himself gains a few secondary advantages from his sense of being rejected; he wins a few skirmishes, takes what compensations he can and subjects others to his will. But these are short-term victories – flashes of lightning in the sky before the impending storm.

Let me tell you a story ...

Grandparents are always a great asset

Three-year-old Laura sat in the back seat of her parents' car, surrounded by parcels and packages. In her pink summer dress, she too looked as if she needed careful wrapping, with the word "fragile" on the parcel.

After a longish journey, they arrived at her grandparents' house in town.

It was a great joy to see Grandma and Granddad again and receive the presents they had prepared for her. Grandma showed Laura her delightful little bedroom and immediately began unpacking her suitcases and parcels.

When evening came, her parents got back in the car, having kissed Laura over and over again.

"We'll come and fetch you soon," said her father.

"Don't cry," begged her mother.

But Laura had no intention of crying, because she did not really understand what was happening.

When night fell, Laura let her grandmother put her to bed, let her sing her nursery rhymes and smooth her hair. But when her grandmother thought she had finally lulled Laura to sleep, the little girl stood bold upright on the bed and stated imperiously: "I want Mummy!"

Her grandmother was not in the least taken aback. She said gently: "I know you do. Mummy will be coming."

"I want her straight away," demanded Laura.

"Mummy has had a lovely idea; she has left me to look after you in her place."

Laura looked at her quizzically.

"You know that Mummy trusts me, because I was her mummy when she was a little girl, a little girl like you."

Laura's brow became more furrowed still.

"And," her grandmother added merrily, "she has given me something to show you that she is very, very near." She opened the wardrobe and took out a tiny night-light.

"Look, this is what Mummy left to keep you company."

Laura's eyes had already filled with tears but she held them back. They remained there, on the edge, awaiting their mistress's orders. Meanwhile, Laura examined the mysterious little light, which was a soft green colour. Her grandmother turned out the big light and the night-light seemed even more mysterious.

"Mummy is there," concluded Laura and she went to sleep.

Days and days went by and the summer was over. Her father and mother had made just two short visits, on the day the hotel was closed. It had been a very good season in their village high up in the valley. Even though their hotel was new and not well known, they had had many guests staying. But they still had many debts to pay off and, apart from a cook, they were not yet able to take on other staff.

They took Laura home for a week. Her mother found time to cuddle her and give her attention, then one day she said: "Shall we go to Grandma's again?"

Laura's face clouded over a little: "And what about you? Will you come, too? And Daddy?"

"We'll come with our little princess; we'll spend a day all together; but then we'll have to come back here and work. Grandma and Granddad are very pleased that you will be spending some more time with them. Without you, they feel rather lonely."

Laura had no doubt about this because, when she was at her grandparents', she felt she was the centre of attention and they never had her out of their minds for an instant. On the other hand, when she was at home in the village, at the hotel, her mother and father were always extremely busy.

Laura went back to live with her grandparents, who were looking forward to her return and almost scolded her for staying away so long. Autumn had come and Laura attended nursery school for the first time. She really enjoyed it. In the morning, her grandfather would take her to school, stopping off at the café to buy her a cake while he had his coffee. In the afternoon, her grandmother was always waiting in the front row and, the moment the teacher opened the door, she would embrace Laura and say: "At last. I've been missing you so much."

Laura's mother and father came to visit at least twice a month, on the day the hotel was closed. She looked forward to their visits as one looks forward to a party; she always had so many things to show them.

"Mummy has said you must stay away from school when she comes with your father," her grandmother announced happily.

Those were wonderful days.

"How you've grown!" her father would say. "Grandma and Granddad must be looking after you well!"

Laura needed no convincing, but her grandmother insisted on adding: "You've done well, too, in trusting us. This dear little girl is the light of our life – even when she is a bit naughty."

During Laura's second year at nursery school, one day her best friend asked her a strange question: "But haven't you got a mother and a father?"

"Yes, of course I have!" answered Laura firmly.

"I've never seen them. I only ever see your grandparents."

"I live with my grandparents," admitted Laura.

"Have they left you alone with your grandparents, then?" persisted her friend.

"Alone with my grandparents? I'm not alone with my grandparents!" answered Laura, amazed at the idea that one might be alone in the company of one's grandparents.

"I see," said her friend, bowing to the facts, "my mother said you had no parents."

"I do have parents and they love me very much; my grandma told me so."

"I see."

And that was the end of the conversation.

But a slight doubt was implanted in Laura's heart.

"Doesn't Mummy want me?" she asked her grandmother, whom she trusted very much.

"Of course, she loves you!" her grandmother replied without a moment's hesitation. "You are her life; she often tells me so."

Laura opened her eyes really wide, in a special way she had.

"When you're a bit bigger, you'll be able to go home and live with Mummy and Daddy – when you've learned to look after yourself a bit more."

"And what about you?" asked Laura immediately.

"You greedy little thing!" said her grandmother, smiling. "You'd like to have everyone all the time, wouldn't you?"

"Yes."

"But that's not possible, silly! Now you've got your grandparents here; then you'll have your parents there at home."

"And will you and Granddad come and see me?"

"Of course we will. In fact, you know what? When we are really old and we can't look after ourselves any more, would you have us to live with you at your house?"

"Oh, yes!" said Laura, hugging her grandmother.

Things to talk about with your child
- Why does Laura say she's not alone with her grandparents?
- Why are her grandparents grateful to her?
- Laura is convinced that her mummy and daddy love her. Why?

Chapter Eight

When one parent "steals" the other

Case study

David was his father's greatest supporter. Aged eleven, he had "chosen" to stay with his father rather than go with the other half of his family: his mother and his two-year-old sister Lisa. David knew "everything", because his father treated him like a man – an ally or companion. He had witnessed the "tragedy" (a term his father used very, very often); his father had finally realised that David's mother was coming home late in the evenings on account of the office manager. At first, she had tried to conceal the fact: "It's not true! You're just thinking badly of me! It's just that there's so much to do at the office at this time of year; we're getting ready for the furniture show. If we don't give it our all, we shall lose business to rival firms. It's the most important time of year for the company, you know."

"Well, I get home from the office punctually at 6 p.m., which means I have to look after the children, prepare the dinner and even put them to bed."

"Look, it won't be for long. If you're tired, why don't I ask my mother to keep them during the evening as well?"

"No, no, I don't mind the children; in fact, David is very helpful. It's just that I like you to be at home."

"Yes, you're right. But I can't take it easy for the time being."

"Well then, what's more important, your job or your family?"

"Please try to understand. I'm just asking you to be patient for the next few weeks."

"But are you sure that's all there is to it?"

"If you start being jealous, we'll never be able to get on."

Discussions of this kind were an everyday occurrence. It was no good David turning up the volume of the television, concentrating on the cartoons and pretending not to hear; the strident arguments penetrated his defences and constantly troubled his mind.

Then, one evening, all hell broke loose.

"You liar, you whore, you good-for-nothing; I've got proof that I was right!" shouted his father in a flood of tears.

And, at the same time, he thrust a crumpled letter in his wife's face: "This is a love letter from your boss!"

"You've been searching among my private things?" she yelled in return.

"Yes, I have. I would never have learned the truth from you!"

"I knew it, you're a pig! You don't respect me! I asked you to give me time; now you've ruined everything."

"I've ruined everything?" cried his father. "It's you that's destroyed our marriage."

"Yes, it's a marriage that's been on the rocks for years. If you must know, in my boss I've found everything I didn't find in you."

"But you said he was old and bald and insensitive ... Or were you just saying it to pull the wool over my eyes?"

"He's a real man and he really looks after me."

"You, go to bed," said his father suddenly, turning to David.

"No, I won't!" exploded David and ran to hug his father's knees. "Poor Daddy!"

His mother had turned her head away, as if she did not want to see, saying almost to herself: "So, you've turned him against me."

His father was talking, shouting, crying, threatening, begging. And suddenly they passed the point of no return; she dialled a number on her mobile phone and ordered: "Come and pick me up."

From that moment on, her face was a hard mask. She threw a few things into a couple of suitcases and went out, into the dark of the night, as soon as she heard her boss's car draw up.

David's father hugged his son tightly, sobbing: "Mummy has gone and left us."

He took David to their double bed, while little Lisa slept alone in her bedroom.

Next morning, soon after their father – almost exhausted from crying and a sleepless night – had phoned the office to say he would not be going to work, their mother turned up, saying nothing. She found another two suitcases to pack essential items for their daughter and, as she was loading them into the car with her husband looking on as if paralysed, turned to David and said: "Do you want to come with me?"

"No," said David, his tone dull and lifeless. He was certain at that moment that he could not even consider leaving his father alone.

In the days that followed, there was talk of solicitors, court hearings, divorce, settling of property and agreed visiting times – not just days but months and months of unbearable tension.

David did all he could to comfort his father, even doing his homework on his own.

"Look, your child has become such a hard worker, poor little chap; I no longer need to persuade him to do his homework," said his grandmother, when his father – on time as always – came to pick him up.

His grandmother, as David was well aware, was his mother's mother; and she too was at a loss as to what could be done to remedy the situation. She said to her son-in-law: "You didn't deserve to suffer a blow like this. But we'll see what happens."

The pair of them would exchange information as to his mother's doings: she telephoned; she spent five minutes on the phone to David or she immediately put the phone down because he answered in monosyllables; she was interested in what his father said to her or she was not interested; she was seen with "him" in a car. Then there was what the neighbours were saying; how "others" received the news; whether they should go and talk to the parish priest and David's teachers or if it would be better to wait. They were like a pair of dogs with a bone. It was as if the most exciting thing in life was keeping tabs on David's mother.

"And if she returns, shall we have her back?" his father asked David.

"Yes," said David shrilly, though he felt that his answer alarmed his father slightly.

Meetings with David's mother were a real problem.

"I don't want her to take David to her place when he's there," grumbled David's father to his mother-in-law.

"You're quite right. He won't learn anything good from him."

David's father was immovable on this point and resisted all his former wife's objections: "But how can I keep David for a whole day without letting him in? You know we're living together now, don't you? And, in any case, it doesn't concern you, now that we're separated."

"What happens to my son does concern me!" hissed his father.

"Aren't you just being your usual repressive and overbearing self? In any case, Lisa lives with us; isn't she your child, too?"

"If you hadn't taken her away ... In any case, when I take Lisa out for the day I bring her here and she spends the time with me and her brother, in a happy environment ..."

"What! You mean my home is not happy?"

And the quarrelling began all over again.

Of course, when David came home after his fortnightly meeting with his mother, his father gave him the third degree.

"What did you do?"

"Mummy took me to the park, then to the supermarket, then she left me to have lunch at Grandma's, because she had to cook for him, then she picked me up again, then ..., then ..."

"Did you see him?"

"No; or rather, just for a moment, when he was leaving the house 'to get out of the way', as Mummy put it."

David tried every possible way of consoling his father. The only thing he had kept for himself were his football training sessions, though he wanted his father to be there, especially when he was playing in a match. He would say: "It's not the same if you don't come to watch"; and his father would think: "What a good thing I've got him; if not I'd have thrown myself under a train." Apart from his football, David had given up everything: afternoons spent with friends, the idea of joining the scouts, his own amusements. What did it matter if his father hardly noticed? The fact was that concern for his father completely filled his mind. David kept a close eye on him, asking him with an almost motherly solicitude: "What's the matter?" when he saw he was a bit down or depressed.

When David spent the day with his mother, she never asked him how his father was. David would have liked to talk to her about him and sometimes tried to do so, but she rebuffed him with: "Forget about Daddy; now you're here with me."

She tried to cuddle him, as well as encouraging him to "behave in a way appropriate to his age" – as she put it – because she was worried that his father demanded too much of him (and she knew only too well how obsessive and overbearing his father could be!).

The summer came and his mother – claiming her "right" – took David to her new husband's house in the mountains, together with Lisa, having given copious assurances that "he" would not be there.

However, "he" turned up the very next day, "just to teach us how to look after ourselves in the mountains, because otherwise the three of us might get into danger".

During those magical days, away from the everyday grind, David seemed to soften towards his mother and did not resist the presence of her new husband. His father phoned him every evening, but David never said anything about "him" being there.

After a time, David even found he was beginning to like this discreet and self-confident man, who had bought him some grown-up boots for rock-climbing. Strangely enough, he found himself forgetting his father, sometimes for half a day at a time.

When his mother took him back home, he had a healthy sun-tan and looked more carefree and relaxed.

His father looked at him apprehensively: "Did you have a good time with your mum?"

"Yes, I did," he said with a smile, "we went for lots of walks, we ate at a restaurant and we went to the leisure centre. It was great."

His father looked worried and asked further questions. His former wife admitted that "he" had been present, because she feared that the boy would confess it in any case. His father was mortified: "What! He was there, too, and you didn't tell me!" he said, going pale. He did not add: "You've betrayed me; you've deceived me; you've hurt me; I would not have believed it; you're cruel to me." He never uttered these words, because he knew in his heart that he had no right to; but they were clearly written on his face.

David suddenly felt monstrously guilty; he could not even trust himself!

How the father would defend his conduct

As we distance ourselves from this painful story of separation and conflict, we cannot suppress a very strong feeling that nobody – not even in the most distressing circumstances – has the right to make use of a child in this way. Let us call a spade a spade: this is psychological abuse; and it will have weighty consequences for the future development of the child.

Of course – and this is not to excuse them – both parents would be astonished to hear their behaviour described in this way and would deny it with all their strength. Let us imagine what the father would say in reply to this accusation: "You're exaggerating. I'm the one who has been abused. My wife has gone off and abandoned us. I have devoted myself exclusively to my son; I've had no ulterior motive; I haven't wanted anything else. I've never left him on his own, poor child, abandoned by his heartless mother. I've tried to compensate for her absence in every possible way; I have not denied him affection, attention or friendship. How can you make such an accusation? I haven't even set him against his mother; on the contrary, I've kept to the agreement and encouraged him to spend time with her, without trying to hold him back. I'm above reproach; or are you criticising me because I've tried to protect my son from the intrusions of that other man? Perhaps you think I shouldn't try to bring him up with principles? In any case, it's not my fault if he has taken it all in; the 'tragedy' happened before his very eyes. Was I supposed to tell him lies? They are the ones who are teaching him to tell lies, like the time I let him go to the mountains. David – sensible boy that he is – understands perfectly well what his mother has done.

"Is he on my side? Well, yes, he is; but could it be otherwise, given that he has eyes to see the way things have happened? On the other hand, I've made him feel that he is important to me; I've given him reasons for going on living. I don't call that abuse!"

How the mother would defend her position

Now let us try to imagine what his mother would say: "I can't be blamed for making a new life for myself; no one could have expected me to go on living with that man, who always oppressed me. When at last I found some one who really loved me, I was entitled to think of my own needs. I certainly haven't neglected my children; I kept the little one with me, because she was too young to be exposed to her father's negative influence. In David's case, his father simply set him against me; only I know how much I have suffered from his hostility. His father and my mother have robbed me of his affection. And yet, I've done everything possible to get close to him and show him that there is a place for him, too. In any case, he's a bit older; it's up to him to realise what's going on and decide for himself. There was nothing more I could do.

"Many times I have been tempted to set him against his father, in order to have him with me, but I have resisted the temptation, because I knew it would be too painful for my son to tear himself away from his father. Can I be said to have abused him because, during the holidays, I didn't fall in with his father's absurd wishes that my partner should not be there? How can someone be so ridiculous? I realised how stupid it was when David finally relaxed, began to enjoy himself and felt he was part of the family. If anyone has been abusing him, it's his father!"

An egocentric, distorting filter

Of course, we do not know if David's father and mother would defend themselves in this way when really faced with the (admittedly, involuntary) abuse their son has suffered. But the fact is that in self-justifying arguments of this kind we find the violent root of this sort of child abuse, consisting in an inability to see things from the child's point of view.

Let us say that every situation of serious marital conflict and/or separation is potentially violent and abusive for the children; and the more monstrously selfish the adults are, the more they are the prisoners of their own point of view, the worse the abuse is likely to be. The adults are wrapped up in their own hurt, disappointment, resentment and desire for revenge and see the child only through this filter. This is when abuse occurs. Both parents think that the child could not but be on their side (not – please note – on their side as a parent, but as a partner) if the other parent had not the power to set the child against them.

And so, while with the merest shreds of good faith both parents excuse themselves for subversive manoeuvres against the other, they are blind to the fact that the demand they are really making – by implication at least – is: "If you are on my side, you cannot (must not) be on the side of the other."

Any parental separation is by definition a source of hurt for the children. Their security stems from the "we" of the couple, from the perceived bond between mother and father. Moreover, they have a vague sense of bearing something of the father and something of the mother within themselves. When forced to suffer their separation, they run the risk of believing that part of themselves is being (or has to be) amputated.

The real violation consists in asking a child (more or less explicitly!) to be on the side of one against the other. It is as if the parent were saying: "If you agree with my reasons, you can't agree with those of the other"; "If you think I am wrong, you must certainly think that the other is right"; "If you want my unconditional approval, you can't seek it from the other at the same time." And so, as well as the pain of losing the "we" on which his or her security was based, the child must bear another, enormous burden: that of being on one side or the other.

"I didn't ask him to take sides," observed one mother, "he did so of his own free will." When asked why he would have taken her part in this spontaneous way, the mother had no hesitation in replying: "Because he can see I'm right (!) and because he can feel how much I am suffering. But I certainly did not ask him to be angry with his father." In other words, the parent is asking the child to see things through her eyes, in which there is no room for doubt. This is shocking!

That is not all. It is now becoming orthodox doctrine (thanks to social workers, marriage counsellors, etc.) that it is not right to set a child against the other parent. But when the heady fog of resentment thickens, only lip-service tends to be paid to this principle. The parent may well make a show of saying: "You must understand that your father/mother loves you; he/she has his/her good points; I don't want to set you against him/her!" But these are mere words, which can be very confusing, because the child senses that behind the words there is no true respect or, at least, no attempt to understand how the lack of respect threatens everything the other does for his or her child. What is urgently needed is family counselling which generates a (revolutionary) new understanding of the need for mutual trust, not between the parents as a couple but in their acting as parents for the good of the child. The child's inner resources cannot be activated unless he or she is helped not to take sides. This requires a "parental alliance" – and this, I repeat, is something that can be learned.

Otherwise, the disadvantaged children will tend to transform their disadvantage into a temporary advantage by trying to obtain something from one parent when they cannot get it from the other; when one parent acts in a strict or inconvenient way, they will take refuge on the other bank.

But these short-term gains will have even more harmful long-term effects: "In any case," the little navigator may conclude, "I don't really trust anyone."

Taking sides for eternity

An even more disastrous situation can arise. This happens when children who have taken sides on the basis of their gut feelings then change their position, maybe without realising it, maybe because it is to their advantage to do so. They will never forgive themselves if the parent to whom they are attached shows them that he or she is "mortally wounded" by their change of position. Little David, trapped into complicity with his mother in not telling his father that the mother's new partner is with them on holiday, discovers a new aspect of things which does not square with his interpretation of the situation up to that point: a mother who has betrayed and abandoned him and his father, a totally unworthy partner, a sister who is "unfortunate" because she is being brought up by her mother. At a certain point, he sees that this picture is not entirely true and maybe for this reason he says nothing about the new partner's being present.

His father exacts a high price for his change of position. The price David pays is not just that he can no longer trust the adult world; now he can no longer even trust himself – a disaster for his future life.

Ensuring real protection for the child

Maybe we have stressed very strongly the violence committed when a child is asked to take sides in so painful a situation as a marital breakdown. Of course, this insistence is in itself insufficient to protect the child; unless a real desire to protect their child arises in the parents' hearts, our protests are sterile. However, it may help to bring to light somewhat less traumatic situations in which the same harmful demand is concealed – any situation in which someone tries to turn the child into a partisan. The child may be incited to take the part of mother against grandmother; paternal aunt against mother; maternal uncle against father; father's parents against mother's parents; brother against sister; father against brother, and so on, following the monotonous human tendency to divide, judge and manipulate.

A child who is obliged to take sides is a child on whom an additional – monstrously unnecessary – hurt is inflicted.

Let me tell you a story ...

The keyboard

Frederick was the most miserable child in the world: his father had gone away and he was left with his mother and elder sister. He had done all he could to keep his father from going. Although he was only eight years old – very young for such serious matters – he had understood that Mummy and Daddy were going to get a divorce. He had conducted his own careful investigation: "Don't you both sleep in the big bed any more?"

"No," his mother had replied, holding back her tears.

"Shall I join you, then?" the little hero had immediately suggested, ready to make a sacrifice.

"No," his mother answered firmly, "no one can take Daddy's place."

One evening, wearing his pyjamas, he had jumped out of bed, despite his sleepiness. His father had just come in and was opening out the settee in the sitting-room to make a bed.

Frederick plucked up his courage: "Daddy, you shouldn't sleep here alone. Go in with Mummy."

His father smiled sadly: "She doesn't want me."

"Yes, she does want you!" affirmed Frederick. Then, doubting slightly, he suggested almost to himself: "I'll go and ask her."

"But she's asleep ..."

"It doesn't matter!" or so it seemed to our little hero.

He switched on the big light, without preamble. His mother opened her eyes, wondering what was going on: "What's the matter? What's happening?"

"It's me, Mummy."

"Oh, Frederick, aren't you asleep?"

"No ... Daddy's in the sitting-room ... Can't he come and sleep with you?"

Instead of answering, his mother leapt out of bed and went into the sitting-room, followed by her son: "What sort of behaviour is this? If you want to come back to bed with me, just say so; don't get a child to do your dirty work."

"I didn't send him ..."

"Really? It was all his own idea?"

"Yes," said Frederick honestly.

"You be quiet and get to bed; this is a matter for grown-ups."

A total disaster.

At this point, Frederick finally understood that it was nothing to do with him.

However, when his father packed his bags and left, at least Frederick could tell himself he had tried to keep them together.

All children want to keep their parents together; what they don't usually realise is that it is not their job to do so.

There is a second thing children don't know when their parents separate: their mother is still their mother and their father is still their father. Frederick was not clear on this point. In fact, when his father came to see him, he tried to be nasty to him in every way he could. Should you or should you not punish a father who has gone off and left you – and left you alone with two women? This, at least, was his provisional point of view.

So, when his father arrived, he would pretend that he had other things to do, especially on a Saturday afternoon: "I've arranged to go and play with my friends," he would say importantly. He appeared so heavily engaged, it wouldn't have been surprising if he had consulted his diary (something he had learned from his father).

"Can't you play with them tomorrow?"

"No, I've arranged it for today."

"If you come with me, I'll buy you a nice ice-cream."

"I don't like ice-creams."

"Since when have you not liked ice-creams?"

"Since I decided not to!"

His father almost managed to disarm him: "Maybe we could see a nice film, with a cartoon …"

"You're kidding …" said Frederick, trying not to believe it, despite the excitement in his eyes.

His mother, standing in the background, never intervened.

"But why don't you want to come out with me?" asked his father.

His mother shrugged, as if to say: "I didn't get us into this mess." And Frederick felt his mother's anger and sadness in his own heart.

One day, his father turned up with an electronic keyboard – the very thing he had always wanted. In other circumstances, it would have been a dream come true. Instead, he took the still unopened keyboard and hid it away in a corner of his bedroom cupboard.

"Don't you want us to play with the keyboard?" asked his father disappointedly.

"No."

Frederick could not be bought. The only present he really wanted was for his father to come back home. Otherwise, he could not allow himself to be happy.

Months went by in this way and the pain in his heart did not go away.

Then, one day, his mother sat him on her lap and said: "Listen, little man, it's pointless you pretending you haven't got a father. You have got a daddy and he loves you."

"That's not true, because he's not here with us."

"He can't live here, because it's all over between the two of us; but he's still your father."

"But he left me!"

"No, he left me, not you. Just think, every month he pays a lot of money into my bank account for you and your sister."

"Why?"

"To look after you, to provide for all your needs. The judge set the figure, but I am sure that he would pay the money anyway, even if he did not have to."

"You mean he goes out to work for me?"

"Yes, little man, partly for you."

"And he loves me?"

"I've already told you, he loves you very much. You could perhaps show him your exercise books when you get a good mark. He is proud of you. He phones you every day, doesn't he?"

"Yes."

"Well, sometimes you could phone him."

More time went by. Frederick did not phone his father himself, but he ran to speak to him when his father phoned. Then, one day, when he decided the time was right, he opened his wardrobe, took out the keyboard and looked at it carefully. When he started to play it, a great weight was lifted from his heart.

His mother, attracted by the strange music, came into his room and kissed him. Yes, Frederick had two parents again.

Things to talk about with your child
- Why was Frederick so miserable?
- What convinced him that his father was still his father?
- And was his mother still his mother?

Chapter Nine

When a parent is impossible to please

Case study

Irma had no doubt that she was her mother's pride and joy. They lived in a foreign country, where people spoke a language different from the one they spoke at home, but what did it matter? She was the centre of her mother's world. None of her friends at school wore such dazzling clothes as Irma did. Her mother was a born seamstress; all she needed was a brightly coloured piece of material and she would sew the most original, charming dress, often adorned with lace, ribbons and contrasting cuffs and lapels. In short, she was a genius with a needle.

Wearing the smocked dress her mother had embroidered, Irma felt like a princess. Her mother would go into town and find inspiration in the shop-window displays; she was certainly not going to waste her money buying ready-made clothes for her daughter! She would copy the pattern and improve upon it. And so Irma was undoubtedly the best-dressed girl in her class; not even the greatest German tailor could have given his creations that special Mediterranean tone, which spoke of sunshine, colour, vitality and *joie de vivre*. Irma's clothes seemed to have power to transform the greyness of the Northern European environment – or so, at least, she thought.

"What did the German girls say to you?" her mother would ask when her daughter came home from school. She spoke the words "German girls" with an unmistakable nuance, as if to say "those foreigners", "rivals", representatives of another world that was to be envied and competed with. Her attitude was a mixture of expectation, ambition, rivalry and fear.

Her mother would make Irma put on her latest creation, then stand her in front of the mirror, place her hands on her shoulders and gaze at her reflection, as if wanting to transform her: "We'll show those German girls. You'll outshine them all! We'll show them what Italian women are made of. You'll be second to none. You'll marry a rich, handsome man; you'll be received in all the best homes; you'll amaze them all with your elegance."

Irma would also gaze at herself in the mirror, until she did not know if she was seeing herself through her own eyes or those of her mother.

Sometimes, during these same day-dreaming sessions, her mother would say: "Your father went to speak to your teachers – he's learned a few sentences of German at work – and they told him that you speak the language perfectly, better than a native-born German. And your homework is always faultless. I was right not to send you to the Italian school, among all those people the Germans look down on as ragamuffins. You'll be our vindication, my little one!"

Irma had no doubt that she was the apple of her parents' eye. When she came home with a "1" for her work – the top mark, which often not even her German friends were awarded – her mother was astonished: "One! What sort of mark is that? I only studied until sixteen back home, but there the top mark was ten – and no one ever got it!"

"Here, the top mark is one, Mummy."

"These Germans have got everything upside down, but you'll beat them all!" And she would hug Irma tightly, cuddle her and stroke her hair, cover her with kisses and say: "You're all I've got."

Then Irma's little heart was full of joy and love for her mother.

But a few weeks later, her mother's behaviour could be quite different.

Irma would return home with some new trophy in her satchel and her mother would not so much as look at it. She was lying on the settee, her thoughts miles away.

"Mummy …"

"What? Leave me alone. There's something to eat on the table."

Irma would sit down at the table, eat whatever she found, then clear up in silence. Sometimes there was no food at all … In that case, she would adopt the German custom, spreading black bread with butter and sliced cheese. She would eat in silence while watching her mother, who lay there with her eyes closed.

"Mummy … What's the matter?"

"Nothing. I've got a headache. Don't make a noise."

Irma would settle down quietly to do her homework, which was the only thing she could do to suppress her unhappiness.

Then, a few hours later, she would switch on the television: "Switch it off," her mother would whine. "I can't bear to hear that barbarian drivel."

Irma would switch off the television, not knowing what to do. Sometimes she would try and approach her mother and stroke her hair, but the result was always unpredictable. Sometimes her mother would say, in an unhappy, self-pitying voice: "Oh, my little treasure. What would I do without you?" But she might snap back: "Leave me alone! Leave me alone!"

Finally, at the end of his shift, which might not be until 10 p.m., her father would arrive home.

"Mummy's got a headache."

"Again?" her father would reply; and Irma felt as if his words were a reproach.

"Yes, I've no strength to do anything … no desire …"

"Stay there, then, and I'll organise things," said her father, in a way that Irma found hard to interpret. So her father would try to tidy up, put something on to boil and do the washing up. Then he would say to Irma: "Let's go to bed; tomorrow I've got to get up at 5 a.m."

Her father often did two shifts in a twenty-four-hour period.

Her mother might not even bother to move from the settee, asking him to give her some more blankets: "It's so cold here … so rare to see the sun … that's why I'm ill. You brought me here to suffer …"

"But you know there was no work back home," he replied.

"That was because you didn't go out and look for it … You just hung around waiting to go abroad, like your brothers …"

"We'll go back when we've made a pile of money and build our own house …"

"Oh yes, I'll be dead by then …"

Often, though, her father did not even reply, preferring to withdraw into his own inner world. For Irma, the days were endless. Of course, she could not ask to go out and play with her German friends and she had lost touch with nearly all the Italian girls she knew.

Time went by and her sun would suddenly reappear, though it might be foggy outside. Her mother would begin sewing her dresses again; Irma's heart would again beat more strongly and again things were wonderful. Her mother's Neapolitan songs seemed to penetrate the walls, even getting into the furniture and drawers. And then a relative or neighbour might come and call – but only then, because "on her bad days" Irma's mother could not bear to have anyone around. Sometimes she would cook an Easter cake, getting Irma to help her.

Once she even sent Irma to school with some and all the class loved it. The teacher asked Irma for the recipe, but her mother's mind was made up: "The Germans could never make an Easter cake!"

Once, however, Irma arrived home in tears; a fellow pupil had teased her because of her Italian origins. But as Irma began to tell her what had happened, her mother brushed her story aside: "Oh, that's nothing to get upset about. You shouldn't cry about little things like that." And although the strains of "O sole mio" were wafting through their living room that day, somehow they did not bring joy to Irma's heart.

Then the times when her mother "had no strength" would begin all over again. And then none of the good things that were happening to Irma made any impression on her mother. Even when, at the end of the school year, Irma was awarded a prize, her mother's only reaction was a joyless "Oh yes?"

At these times, Irma would write little notes to her mother – notes that cost her a great effort because she was now more accustomed to writing in German.

She would write several notes a day: "Mummy, I love you," and she framed the words with coloured hearts, exclamation marks and other bright patterns.

It did not achieve the desired effect.

So Irma redoubled her efforts, writing more – and longer – letters: "Mummy, I love you very, very much"; "Mummy, I love you lots"; "Mummy, your little girl loves you more than anything in the world"; "Mummy, tell me you love me. Your daughter loves you so much"; "You are my best mummy ever, I love you very much." All signed: "Your sweet Irma." Sometimes her mother would make the effort to read them; sometimes she just dropped them with a sad smile.

Gradually Irma began to "understand": it was she who was in the wrong. Her mother would say: "I've got a headache," but Irma could read the underlying message; she was not able to make her mother happy!

This became more and more obvious to her. When she was told to hang up the washing on the line at the other end of the room, she could never get it right. From the settee, her mother would say: "Not like that! You don't hang shirts by the sleeves."

Irma tried and tried again.

"Before hanging the pillowcases you have to shake them out; else they'll dry with creases in them. And then the socks have to be hung up in pairs, first the darker ones, then the lighter ones ..."

Little Irma strove to do her best, but when she went to take the clothes down, some of them were bound to be creased. Her mother would sigh: "I have to do everything in this household!"

And, after Irma had struggled for hours to hang everything up properly, her mother might still get up with an apparently superhuman effort and hang the whole wash up all over again.

There were just so many things Irma could not do well. She felt it was she who was at fault. She was incapable of pleasing her mother. The fact that her father was also unable to please his wife was no consolation. On the contrary, it made her try all the harder – but in vain – to satisfy her. She at least must make her mother happy. But she failed at every attempt.

When the family becomes a gas chamber ...

We would all like to think that this story is blown up and exaggerated (and that includes me!), but in my work I have come across situations even worse than this one. And such situations arise not only when there is a language barrier between the home and the outside world but also in our own cities and towns. They arise when a parent demands to be consoled and remains inconsolable; when a parent asks a child to make him or her happy and yet is impossible to please. This triggers a dreadful and unending secret game; the more the child tries to please the parent, the more he or she is frustrated. Effectively, the parent is saying: "You still have not done enough." It is unlikely that a child will have the clarity of mind to let go; it is almost impossible for the child to think: "The fact Mummy or Daddy is impossible to please is not my fault." No, the child tries and tries with all his or her strength and – in all probability – the parent will be tempted to take the game a little further, encouraging the child with the bait: "Just a bit more and you'll get there!"

... without doors or windows giving access to other families

We can never emphasise enough that the family is not self-sufficient; it cannot cope alone in fighting the inner demons of mistrust, fear, anxiety and lack of understanding.

What is needed is not only a policy of financial support for the family (essential though that may be), but a network of solidarity and psychological and social support so that the family does not have to create its own social world out of nothing.

The church also has an important role to play; what are its members doing to safeguard and prosper the sacrament that should bind two children of God?

The purpose of this little tract is to bring to light and alleviate the suffering of children or, at least, to make us aware of the ways in which we tend to exacerbate such suffering.

It is obvious that no parent is expected to create a completely self-contained oasis for his or her child. To all intents and purposes, the child is a child of that family, that culture, that society. The reality principle applies to him or her as to everyone else and, in any case, the child has his or her own inner resources, provided we are imaginative enough to awaken them. In the case of Irma, it is clear that she is bound to feel the impact of the clash of two cultures, of the family's being foreigners in a foreign land, of the mother's inability to adapt. No one can expect her family to create a gilded oasis for her. Not even the best of parents is able to keep his or her child from experiencing difficulties and suffering.

What we are arguing here is that these unavoidable difficulties are enough; it is wrong for adults to lay further burdens on the child's shoulders!

Three ways in which the care of a child becomes distorted

Let us examine three ways in which the care due to a child becomes distorted.

The first major distortion is ill-treatment in its various forms (abandonment, abuse, violence, sadism, manipulation, paedophilia). We have discussed these phenomena elsewhere[1] and, generally speaking, such forms of ill-treatment (including psychological abuse of the kind described in Chapters Seven and Eight) have been adequately researched. Pathological phenomena in the strict sense of the term do not come within the scope of this book.

Another kind of distortion – "excessive care" – is also fairly well documented. This includes instances in which the parent is obsessive in caring for the child (see the case history in Chapter Four). It may manifest itself in serious anxiety every time a child faces suffering;

mollycoddling; fear whenever the child seeks greater independence; and the "factitious disorder by proxy syndrome", when the child is taken from doctor to doctor until he or she is diagnosed to be ill, dosed up with medicines, and obsessively tested and treated. It is as if the parent were seeking treatment for his or her own anxiety, and fear of being ill, through the child. In other words, the parent devotes himself or herself to playing the role of nurse and ends up requiring the child to take the part of patient. But here, of course, we are again straying into the pathological.

Thirdly, there are distortions of care which we might describe as "miscare": forms of care which are inappropriate, which swing from one extreme to the other, completely overlooking the child's real needs as and when they arise.

The child's real needs

This is what happens to Irma, in two ways at least. First and more generally, there are her mother's mood swings: at one moment, Irma is put on a pedestal, cuddled and spoilt; the next, she is ignored, marginalised and not understood. When she comes home from school, Irma does not know if she will find a mother ready to praise her, find her interesting and make her the centre of her world; or a mother who refuses contact with her and conveys the message: "Try not to exist."

Who is there to tell Irma that her mother is ill; that these violent mood swings are nothing to do with her, a little girl striving to please? Who is there to defend Irma, to provide her with the "protective garment" that would insulate her from these catastrophic changes of mood? Who is there to help her interpret the emotional ups and downs that characterise her relationship with her mother? Certainly not her father, who also seems to be a slave to his wife's changing humour, unable to cope with it except by more or less veiled accusations and clumsy remedies – for instance, taking the child to bed and leaving his wife to sleep on the settee. And who is there to tell this husband that his wife is ill, that she needs treatment?

A more specific aspect of this "miscare" is the mother's inability to appreciate Irma's real needs. Clearly, her dressing the child in beautiful clothes so that she outshines her school friends is not in response to a need expressed by Irma. It is a symptom of the mother's own need, which she seeks to satisfy through the child, launching her into the world to compensate her for her own hurts.

In this case study, there are two points at which the "miscare" I refer to is particularly evident. When the child comes home feeling hurt because she has been devalued and marginalised (for being Italian), her mother plays down what has happened, apparently insensitive to her daughter's suffering; she conveys the message that it is something in Irma that is not right. Then, when the child expects her mother to be overjoyed because she has won a prize, her mother is "absent in spirit" because of her illness. Her child's real needs do not enter into her mind.

Blaming oneself as a way of resolving the difficulty

No human being is able to survive in a world so changeable and inconsistent that what is black today is white tomorrow, what seems good today has to be rejected tomorrow, and vice versa. In such circumstances, a child will come up with an interpretation based on his or her egocentrism (the feeling – typical at this age – that he or she is at the centre of things). The child will arrive at the conclusion: "I am the one at fault. It is in me that there is something wrong; I cannot behave myself properly."

When Irma's mother, bound by her obsessions, asks Irma to hang up the washing according to her rigid rules, Irma is not able to refuse; she cannot know – without help – that such demands are abnormal and excessive and are dictated solely by her mother's own inner needs. All she knows is that she is unable to do as her mother wants, unable to perform the services her mother demands so insistently and disturbingly. And her mother's obsessive remedying of the situation (repeating the task she had given to her daughter) is "proof", in the child's eyes, that she is unable to please her. The child will probably develop a whole series of checking mechanisms – of herself and the world about her – to try and make sure she is up to the job; but underneath she will be convinced that her incompetence will become evident every time she is required to do something.

Of course, the child will meet other people in the course of her life and these encounters will save her from the situation of being centred exclusively on a mother she can neither dominate, nor satisfy, nor predict. From this unhappy situation, she may well derive a heightened sensitivity and an ability to be open to others' needs. She will learn certain strategies; think, for example, of the heart-rending tenderness of the notes she writes to console her mother. She may make a wonderful nurse; but let us hope she will have learned the self-confidence without which it is impossible to serve others in a healthy way.

Finally, let us ask ourselves: what have we done to spare potential Irmas – children living out an emotional roller-coaster ride of this kind – the monstrous additional suffering we have introduced into the most important relationships of their lives?

Let me tell you a story ...

A full and complete love

Elena thought she had two mothers; one was called Granny and the other Mummy. Her granny spent the whole day with her, because her mummy went out to work. Her granny did the cooking – and did it very well; her mummy did the washing and ironing – and did it very well.

Elena's father would say: "I'm fortunate I've still got my mother."

It had taken Elena a long time to digest the fact that her granny was her father's mother. Now, though, she was seven years old and was beginning to understand such things.

Addressing himself to Elena's mother, her father would also say: "Aren't we lucky to have a granny who manages things so well?"

Her mother would give a quiet nod of assent.

It was true that Irma's granny was efficiency personified. She drove the car into town, picked Irma up from school and, in the afternoon, took her to her various "activities": music, swimming and catechism classes. She would even have gone over Irma's homework with her.

But Irma wanted her mummy to go through her homework with her, when she came home from work at 7 p.m. She could not say why exactly, but she felt this was Mummy's job.

"Why don't you want me to go through your homework with you?" her granny asked in amazement.

When Elena gave no reply, she was tempted into remarking: "When she gets home, Mummy is tired ..." then gave way with the words, "though she is better at doing homework than I am!"

When Irma's mummy came home, Granny would say, as if to excuse herself: "She's waiting for you to help her with her homework."

As soon as Elena saw that her mother was ready, she would jump onto her knee and her mother understood what she wanted. Happily carrying her daughter, she would move over to the table and, following the usual ritual, would ask: "So, what have we got to do today?"

Concentrating on the task in hand, Elena would get out her homework diary and exercise books and they would set to work. They did not spend more than half an hour on it and it was difficult to know who exactly was actually doing the homework: her mother making suggestions or Elena writing things down. Anyway, Elena could tell that her mother was really pleased.

Meanwhile, Elena's granny hung around in the background, sometimes shaking her head, as if perhaps – though Elena could not really make it out – she thought that mother and daughter were too attached to each other.

On Sundays, Elena's mummy did the cooking, because it was Granny's "day off".

Sometimes, though, her father would take them out to a restaurant: "We both work hard all week; it's not right that you should have to give up your Sunday as well."

On these occasions, Elena's mother was very happy. After the "sung" mass, all four of them would leave the church and walk the short distance to the restaurant, which was run by a friend of her father's.

"I've brought all three of my womenfolk," her father would say, to show that, where women were concerned, there was not much anyone could teach him.

The owner would laugh, sit them at a reserved table with fresh-cut flowers and start to serve a meal "fit for a king"; in any case, her father knew he would not be paying the full price.

At times like these, her father would be totally relaxed, drinking a good wine and becoming quite merry: "I have the Lord to thank," he would say in his Lombard dialect, "that I haven't had to make my women slave away today. You are pleased, aren't you, girls?"

Elena's mummy and granny would laugh; they seemed very relaxed, too.

It really was a day of rest.

However, there were things about which her mother and grandmother did not agree at all. And sometimes they would involve Elena's father, who did not know how to cope when such situations arose. This made Elena feel sad. Thank goodness they did not ask her who was right. If they had, she would have been in great difficulty, because she really loved both her mummy and her granny.

Unfortunately, when the two women did not agree, it was often over something to do with her.

It happened one day at the shoe shop.

"No," said her mummy, "£50 is too much to pay for a child's shoes; it's ridiculous."

"But they're really beautiful," replied her granny, "Look how shiny they are! And they're hand made, like they used to be in the past …"

"I said they're too expensive!"

"I tell you what; you pay £20 and I'll pay £30. I've got my pension, after all. Just look how well they suit her; she looks a real little lady!"

"That's just what I mean. They're too smart; I don't want her to get used to having very expensive things."

It was obvious that her mummy was very annoyed, but her granny seemed not to notice: "Come on, put them on, darling. Your granny will pay for them. You really like them, don't you?"

Elena would have liked to tell the truth: that she was not even aware of what shoes she was wearing when she was playing or studying. But perhaps it was better not to tell the truth out of politeness. So she said nothing.

On that occasion, Elena left the shop wearing the shoes her granny had wanted her to have. Her mother had given up the struggle and let Granny pay for them. Then she had added: "Elena, say thank you to your granny."

"There's no need to," her granny had replied.

Elena had said nothing, but she felt a frostiness in the tone of voice of both women. What had it to do with her?

One day, something very strange happened. It was a Saturday afternoon. Elena had been playing in her room for an hour or so when she went into the living-room in search of a video cassette she wanted to watch. There she found her mummy talking quietly with a friend.

The moment she entered, her mummy called her over to her: "Yes, it's you I want, Elena; come here a minute." Then Elena noticed that her mummy had been crying. Without even giving her the chance to ask why, her mummy asked: "Tell Rosi: who do you love more, your mummy or your granny?"

Elena was thrown into confusion. She glanced around her, perhaps looking for a way out. Her granny was in her own room; there was no one in the kitchen. Elena's little heart was swamped by the enormity of the problem: "If I say Mummy, Granny will cry; if I say Granny, Mummy will be hurt."

As Elena said nothing, her mother tried again: "Go on, you can tell me: do you love your mummy more or your granny?"

"I love my mummy with a full and complete love and my granny with a full and complete love!" Elena suddenly came out with. "What?" asked her mummy in amazement.

"Yes, a full and complete love for both of you!" repeated Elena, smiling at last. Her guardian angel must have come down to put such beautiful words in her mouth.

"Because the love she has for her mummy is different from the love she has for her granny," interpreted her mother's friend Rosie.

"So you love me with a full and complete love!" her mother cried out, happy at last.

The story of this full and complete love came up at table, as they were having supper. Granny was also delighted that her granddaughter loved her with a full and complete love. Her father modestly asked if a full and complete love was reserved for him, too. Elena solemnly affirmed that it was.

The story even found its way out of the house and came to the ears of the parish priest, who said: "Sometimes we have to learn from children. Love is not a pie that can be divided up. They teach us that love, when it is real, reproduces itself rather than shrinking with use." And he was very moved.

> ***Things to talk about with your child***
> – What was Elena's difficulty when she was asked if she loved her mummy or her granny more?
> – How did she cope with the question?
> – Why was her answer so true?

---

[1] M. ZATTONI – G. GILLINI, *Contro il Drago. Abusi sessuali sui minori: storie e itinerari di guarigione* [Fighting the Dragon. Sexual abuse of minors: case studies and ways of healing], Queriniana, Brescia 1998.

Afterword

> ... the inner life of the child, which we adults no longer understand and the richness and sensitivity of which we have so long undervalued (Sigmund Freud).

> We want our children to be able to take their own decisions, but we want them to be decisions we agree with (Bruno Bettelheim).

In this well-written book (and good writing is something not to be taken for granted nowadays) is painted a Michelangelesque fresco of childhood deprived of itself and the dignity of autonomous existence – childhood reduced to the stark light and shade of an ageless Caravaggio crystallised from real-life experience.

The "misfortunes of virtue" here become the "misfortunes of childhood". Sadly, such misfortunes are not unknown to those who, with intelligence and empathy, have to deal with cases – illustrated here with such rigour and calm insight – in which the relationship between child and adult has become pathogenic.

The complex world of the child is depicted here with such clarity that everyone will find at least some of the insights he or she needs. The authors have resisted the temptation to manipulate and patronise and this is complemented by a Freudian capacity to love and work to achieve in parents, and in all concerned, a maturity which is adult and aware, and therefore respectful because it is self-sufficient.

One is finally brought to the understanding that every new-born baby, coming into the world overburdened with others' motivations, expectations and libidinal investments, brings with him or her not only – as Sigmund teaches – his or her sexuality. Children also bear in themselves – we would add here – their intangibility. They are no one's chattel, and it is a sad thing if, by expropriation, they must lose themselves.

This "loss of self" is the present image and future destiny of the child who suffers violence. We will pass over the statistics in silence, but every act of violence (even if "only" psychological) is a *vulnus* for the victim which becomes a *minus* for the world as a whole. It represents a cosmic impoverishment, just as much as when a person dies. When innocence, with its openness to the world, is stolen, the no-longer-Earthly Paradise loses its currency and there remains only (?) a dream of future redemption.

In addition to the necessarily disturbing – but nevertheless illuminating – teaching of this book, the authors give us some real pearls of wisdom, born of experience and universally applicable, when they speak of: "the blind determination with which human beings seem set on complicating their lives", "the umbilical cord of the mobile phone" or "the way some parents interrogate their children conceals the fact that they are wanting to be 'fed'". Or again: "One can walk away while continuing to love, without destroying the other person." At the same time, with the clear ambivalence we find in Catullus, they write: "anxiously wanting her to walk away … but not to walk away" (an unconscious but taut evocation of the anguish of abandonment, the illusory and hidden cement of so many "adult" couples going through a chronic pre-crisis).

Then there is a sadness worthy of Manzoni in such phrases as: "such is the way of the world".

Two key messages need to be stressed above all the others: "working through, accepting and experiencing a bereavement means establishing boundaries" against a suffering that would take over everything, and "allowing a child to express feelings of fear and anxiety". These lay the basis for preventing children turning in on themselves and cutting themselves off in just as total a way. From the authors' Catholic background comes the affirmation: "human beings are not made for suffering". Therefore, "sometimes a child's smile can be the quintessence of sadness" and "adults who are closed to the suffering of a child are adults who are defending themselves" from a suffering that they, too, have experienced and that they do not want to acknowledge, fearing that it may trap them again.

It will be difficult for people to deny the evidence of these truths and go on casually exploiting others like a bull in a china shop.

Despite everything, the theme of suffering remains fundamental. On the one hand, the authors stress its necessity if a person is to grow; on the other hand, they refuse to countenance it when it is not necessary. In this apparent contradiction lies the balance of the book – not forgetting that in this and other ways adults are, in Freudian terms, the offspring of the children they once were.

Emphasising the inescapable centrality of the child, in this volume the authors have abundantly demonstrated and explained the manipulations and projections to which the child is unintentionally subjected and the mechanisms of covering and regression which he or she unwittingly adopts.

In particular, the emblematic situation of Henry calls for profound reflection and daily rereading. In his case, "when suffering becomes a tyrant" and "religion contributes to the sense of guilt", it is necessary to change the present environment in order to save the future of the world. Once at least, let us make it possible to contradict Freud when he says that he is "highly dubious of the happiness of childhood as adults later depict it".

In the end, parents are not always to blame and a child might just be happy – why not?

We are upheld by the certainty of utopia.

Paolo Berruti*

* Specialist in neurology; honorary magistrate of the Court of Appeal, children's section.